THE FERRYMAN OF BRILL

AND OTHER STORIES

W. H. G. KINGSTON

The Ferryman of Brill

W. H. G. Kingston

© 1st World Library, 2007
PO Box 2211
Fairfield, IA 52556
www.1stworldlibrary.com
First Edition

LCCN: 2007934211

Softcover ISBN: 978-1-4218-9683-0
Hardcover ISBN: 978-1-4218-9783-7
eBook ISBN: 978-1-4218-9583-3

Purchase *"The Ferryman of Brill"*
as a traditional bound book at:
www.1stWorldLibrary.com/purchase.asp?ISBN=978-1-4218-9683-0

1st World Library is a literary, educational organization
dedicated to:

- Creating a free internet library of downloadable ebooks

- Hosting writing competitions and offering book publishing
scholarships.

1ˢᵗ World Library Literary Society

Giving Back to the World

"If you want to work on the core problem, it's early school literacy."

- James Barksdale, former CEO of Netscape

"No skill is more crucial to the future of a child, or to a democratic and prosperous society, than literacy."

- Los Angeles Times

"Literacy... means far more than learning how to read and write... The aim is to transmit... knowledge and promote social participation."

- UNESCO

"Literacy is not a luxury, it is a right and a responsibility. If our world is to meet the challenges of the twenty-first century we must harness the energy and creativity of all our citizens."

- President Bill Clinton

"Parents should be encouraged to read to their children, and teachers should be equipped with all available techniques for teaching literacy, so the varying needs and capacities of individual kids can be taken into account."

- Hugh Mackay

Chapters 1 to 4 constitute "The Ferryman of Brill", while the other seven chapters are short stories on their own. All these stories had previously appeared in early volumes of "The Quiver". They were collected and published by Cassell's, who were not Kingston's usual publishers, and the book came out in the year of Kingston's death.

CHAPTER ONE

THE PROTESTANT LOVERS—A RIVAL—
DIEDRICH FINDS HIS FOOTSTEPS DOGGED—
FINDS A FRIEND IN THE FERRYMAN—
THREATENED WITH THE INQUISITION—
FLIES TO SEA

Not far from the broad and slow-flowing river Meuse stands the town of Brill. Flanders, in which it is found, formed at the period to which we refer a province of the dominions belonging to Philip of Spain. It was ruled with no very paternal hand by the Duke of Alva, who resided chiefly at Brussels. He had been employed for several years in burning, hanging, drowning, and cutting off the heads of his loving subjects, and torturing them in a variety of ways, in order to make them dutiful children of the Church of Rome, and of his master, Philip. Not with great success, for they still hated, with an unalterable deadly hatred, both one and the other. Brill at that time was not a populous city, nor did it possess much commercial importance; but it was well walled and fortified, however, and had a most commodious port. The inhabitants were peaceable, well-disposed people, who thought as much of themselves as the citizens of other cities of similar importance are apt to do. Among them was a young merchant—Diedrich Meghem. He had made several voyages of adventure, and was well accustomed to a seafaring life. Now prosperous, and hoping to become wealthy, he was about to settle down as a steady citizen on shore, with the expectation of some day, perhaps, becoming burgomaster of his native city. Diedrich, as young men are apt to do, looked about for a wife to share his good fortune, and had fixed his affections on Gretchen Hopper, a fair and very lovely girl, the daughter of a flourishing merchant. Hopper was supposed to be the possessor of considerable wealth—a dangerous distinction in those days. Duke Alva heard of the merchant Hopper's reputed wealth, and had made a note to take an early opportunity of relieving him of a portion if not the whole of it. Hopper was known to hold the reformed principles, and though he was careful not to intrude his opinions in public, the duke's advisers suggested that there would be no difficulty in bringing up an accusation of heresy against him. Diedrich was an ardent Protestant. His eye had long been fixed on William of Orange as the person best able to lift his country out of the present depressed condition in which she groaned.

Gretchen was a quiet, gentle girl, and she also held to the opinions of her father and her lover, in spite of her gentleness, with a determination in no way inferior to theirs. Gretchen soon found out that the honest, generous-hearted Diedrich loved her, and not long after this discovery she acknowledged to him that he possessed her entire heart. She had, however, other admirers, from whom she might have chosen a husband of a nobler family and of greater wealth than Diedrich. Among other pretenders to her hand was Caspar Gaill, a Fleming of good family, who, however, held to the Romish faith and supported the government of Alva. The merchant Hopper had a great regard for Diedrich, and was well pleased to find that he wished to become his daughter's husband. He at once accepted him as a son-in-law, and gave the young couple his blessing.

"The times are not propitious for marriage, however," he observed. "Matters may mend; they can scarcely grow worse. Gretchen is young, and can wait a little. You must have patience, then, my good friend Diedrich."

Gretchen and her lover passed many pleasant evenings together, though it was considered prudent not to make their intended marriage public. One, however, had watched Diedrich's constant visits to the house, and his heart burned with jealousy.

One evening Diedrich was returning to his home, when, looking over his shoulder on hearing footsteps, he discovered that he was followed. When he walked faster, the stranger proceeded also at the same rate; when he stopped, the stranger stopped; when he went at a slow pace, the stranger slackened his speed. At length, passing a shrine at the corner of a street, before which a bright lamp was kept burning, Diedrich turned sharply round, and found himself standing face to face with the person who had been following him.

"What object have you in dodging my steps?" asked Diedrich, placing his hand on his sword ready to draw.

"As you ask me a question, I will put another to you," said the stranger, also drawing his sword half out of the scabbard. "For what purpose do you visit the house where you have been passing the evening?"

"You put a question to which I positively refuse to reply to any one, and still less to you, Caspar Gaill, for I know you well," answered Diedrich, still further drawing out his sword.

"Then I refuse to answer the question you put to me," said Caspar. "We understand each other, and you may know me henceforth as your enemy."

"A matter of very little consequence," answered Diedrich, in a scornful tone.

The young men parted, but from that day forward Diedrich was aware that his footsteps were constantly followed when he went abroad, especially on the Sabbath, when he was accustomed to attend the meetings of the Protestants held in the city. Still he was too proud and too fearless to alter his mode of proceeding on this account. At night often he saw in the distance a dim figure following him, but which, when he turned round, invariably disappeared.

On one occasion he resolved to pursue the spy, and punish him severely if he could overtake him. Scarcely had he left his home when he observed a figure as usual like a distant shadow coming after him. He walked on for some way, as if indifferent to the circumstance, by gentle degrees slackening his pace, till, as he supposed, his pursuer had approached nearer than usual. He then suddenly turned round, and, darting forward, was close up to the man before the latter made any attempt to escape.

"Why, Diedrich Meghem, you seem to be in a desperate hurry this evening," said a voice he thought he recollected.

"What, Peter Kopplestock, are you my secret pursuer?" he asked, in a tone of surprise.

"It may be so, but I may be your guardian angel," answered the person thus addressed, in a low voice. "I have been wishing to see you without witnesses for some days past, and now the matter brooks of no delay."

"Come to my house, then," said Diedrich; "we can speak there without fear of interruption."

W. H. G. Kingston

"That's the very place it will not be wise for me to go to," said Peter; "if I go there I shall be observed. Do you come to my house. You will find a porch a little to the right of it. Slip in there and remain quiet for a few minutes. Should you be followed at the time, your pursuer will pass by and lose sight of you. Come in an hour hence. It will be dangerous to put off the visit till to-morrow."

Diedrich followed the advice of his friend. He had known Peter Kopplestock from his earliest days. Peter was of no very exalted rank, but he had numerous friends who, not without reason, put confidence in him. His chief occupation was that of a ferryman plying across the river Meuse. He also visited the ships which appeared at the mouth of the river when unable for want of wind to come up to the town, and took provisions off to them, and brought messages on shore. Peter Kopplestock took an especial interest in Diedrich; Diedrich had always been his generous employer, and was now going to marry his niece.

The wealthy merchant Hopper had once been a humble clerk, and he then had married the very beautiful sister of Peter the ferryman. She had died, and her young daughter had been educated as well as any young lady in the land. Diedrich was well aware of the relationship, and it increased the confidence he felt in Peter, who was also of his own way of thinking—indeed, a more thorough Protestant could not have been found.

Diedrich found his way, at the hour appointed, to Peter Kopplestock's cottage down by the river-side. He saw, when leaving his own house, the usual figure following him, but he hoped, by hiding himself as Peter had advised him to do, to escape from his pursuer. The cottage door was ajar. He pushed it open and entered. Peter welcomed him cordially.

"I have sad news for you, my friend," said the ferryman. "You have been denounced to the Inquisition as a heretic, and your enemies have resolved to take your life. Among them you may reckon Caspar Gaill. He thinks that by getting rid of you he may win the hand of my fair niece."

"How do you know that?" asked Diedrich.

"He told me so himself," said the ferryman. "He is not aware of our connection, and he takes me to be a Romanist. He confides to me his love for Gretchen, if such a fellow has a heart to love, and, in case she should continue to refuse his hand, he engaged me to assist him in carrying her off. A pretty proceeding that would be. However, I did not decline his offer, but told him that I was very sure he was premature in executing his plan; that he must wait patiently, and that by-and-by, should the young lady continue obdurate, he might put it into execution."

"But what do you advise me to do?" asked Diedrich. "I cannot leave Gretchen—I cannot leave my business to ruin and destruction; I would rather remain and brave the worst."

"Tell me, have any of those who have been denounced to the Inquisition escaped from their fangs?" said Peter. "I trow not; then how do you hope to escape death if you remain? Take my advice, my friend; fly while you can, before your wings are clipped. It is a hard thing, I know, for you to leave the girl you love, and it's cruel to neglect a flourishing business which is affording you a handsome income. But you need not lead a life of indolence. You wear a sword, and you have an arm to wield it. You would be welcomed by those bold rovers of the sea, the 'water beggars.' If you offer your assistance to William de la Marck, he will gladly accept it. It would be a glorious thing to assist in liberating your country, and the only aid we can hope for is from the ocean. On shore

W. H. G. Kingston

we cannot withstand the cruel Spaniards, but at sea we may compete with them successfully."

Diedrich sat silent for some time.

"You cast down my hopes just now, but you have again raised them," he exclaimed. "I will go and consult Gretchen. If she urges me to go, I will follow your advice; I am sure that she will remain true to me till I return."

"I wish that I could persuade you to go off at once," said Peter; "your enemies are vigilant, and determined on your destruction, and any moment you may find yourself in their power."

Diedrich promised to be cautious, and to keep as much as possible within the house during the next day, while he would make all the preparation in his power for his speedy departure, should Gretchen approve of his intention.

Peter told him that there was a vessel down the river on the point of sailing. He was acquainted with the captain, who was a warm partisan of the Prince of Orange, and would do his utmost to protect him should he go on board.

Diedrich Meghem was a brave man, but the Inquisition, he knew too well, was not an institution to be trifled with. Poor Gretchen was overwhelmed with grief when she heard of the dangerous position in which Diedrich was placed. She urged him to fly without delay, promising again and again to be faithful to him, and to welcome him as a husband whenever he should return. The merchant Hopper also advised him to leave the country. Diedrich Meghem had made all the arrangements possible with his head clerk and manager, and was still writing busily at his own house, having packed up such articles as he desired to take with him, when Peter

Kopplestock hurried into his room.

"It's time for you to be off at once, my friend," he exclaimed; "this very night the Inquisitors' officers will visit your house, and if they find you, will carry you off to an imprisonment from which, with life, you will never escape. Here, I have brought this large Spanish cloak; throw it over your shoulders and follow me. Your portmanteau and bags I will take care of."

It was already too dark to distinguish people in the streets. Peter led the way down to the river, Diedrich following him. They were quickly on board the ferryboat, but Peter, instead of pulling over to the other bank of the river, rowed down the stream as fast as his arms could urge on the boat. Diedrich stepped on board the vessel, where he was welcomed cordially by the skipper. Peter threw his portmanteau and bag over the bulwarks, and giving him his blessing, pulled back to the town.

W. H. G. Kingston

CHAPTER TWO

AN UNWELCOME SUITOR—GRETCHEN REFUSES TO ACCEPT CASPAR GAILL—CASPAR PLOTS WITH FATHER QUIXADA TO BETRAY THE PROTESTANTS—THE MONK'S TREACHERY

Gretchen was seated in the parlour of her father's house, busily employed in tapestry work—the constant occupation of young ladies in those days, as at present. The merchant Hopper came in; care and thought sat on his brow. His daughter affectionately inquired the cause of his anxiety.

"I cannot tell you, my child," he answered. "It is enough to know that so many of my friends, in various parts of our unhappy land, have been put to death by fire, and sword, and drowning, through the mandates of the tyrant Alva, and who knows what may be our fate in this city? Hitherto we have escaped, but the priests are busy, and are even now trying to ferret out the Protestants. I am thankful that our friend Diedrich escaped; he would certainly otherwise have been seized."

"Oh, Father! I wish you would try and escape too," said Gretchen; "I will accompany you. We can go to England, that land of liberty. If you cannot take any of your wealth with you, I will labour for you there. Surely we shall find friends there, and need not have any fear of starving."

Their conversation was interrupted by a knock at the door, and Caspar Gaill was announced. Both the merchant and his daughter received him coldly. He came dressed in gay attire, and seemed to consider himself in the light of a favoured suitor. Now he spoke to Gretchen, now he turned to her father. Again he turned to the young lady, and urged her to promise to be his.

"You know not the danger to which you are exposed," he observed. "As the wife of a well-known Catholic you will be safe, and I may be able to protect your father. At present he is in great peril. I do not hesitate to tell him so."

The merchant, thanking Caspar for his offer, assured him that he would not bias his daughter.

"My being in peril must not compel her to give her hand where she cannot also bestow her heart. You will not take amiss what I have said, as it arises from no personal ill-feeling towards you."

In vain Caspar pleaded his cause, and at length, with a frown on his brow, and an angry glance in his eye, although honeyed words were on his lips, he took his departure.

Caspar Gaill left the house of the merchant Hopper in no enviable mood. He took his way through the street till he reached the door of a certain religious house or monastery, as it was called, and inquired for a Father Quixada. He was shown into a cell inhabited by a Spanish monk who acted as his father confessor.

"How fares your suit with the pretty Gretchen, my son?" asked the father, who at the same time, however, had observed Caspar's angry look.

The young man shook his head, and replied briefly that he had been refused.

"No hope?" asked the father.

"None," answered Caspar.

"You would have a better chance if the merchant was out of the way," observed the priest.

"Very likely, but he is cautious. It may be no easy matter to get rid of him," answered Caspar.

"Follow my advice, my son, and it can be managed. You have strong suspicions that he is a Protestant. Pretend that you have given up his daughter, but that you desire to be instructed in the new faith. In a short time he will trust you, and if he attends any place of meeting where the Protestants meet, you can introduce me among them. I can disguise myself so that they shall not know me, and I may then not only mark him, but all others who may be present, and inform against them as may be most convenient."

CHAPTER THREE

CASPAR PROFESSES THE PROTESTANT FAITH—
ATTENDS A MEETING—EFFECT OF THE GOSPEL
ON CASPAR—CASPAR, HOWEVER, KEEPS HIS
ENGAGEMENT WITH FATHER QUIXADA—
DOUBTS AND FEARS—THE MONK ATTENDS THE
NEXT MEETING, AND NOTES ALL PRESENT—
CASPAR'S REMORSE—THE SPY AGAIN IN THE
LITTLE COMPANY— CASPAR WARNS THE
INTENDED VICTIMS—TOO LATE—FATHER AND
DAUGHTER IN THE HANDS OF THE
INQUISITION—CONDEMNED—CASPAR DESPAIRS
OF THE RESULT OF HIS WORK—CONSULTS THE
FERRYMAN—BUT NEW PLANS FAIL

Caspar did not at first like this plan. It was treacherous and deceitful, and he must act the part of a spy and a hypocrite to carry it out; but as it was proposed to him by his father confessor, he came to the conclusion that he ought not to hesitate about it.

The merchant Hopper was surprised a few days after this to receive a visit from Caspar Gaill. The young man told him that he had abandoned all hopes of winning his daughter's hand; indeed, he thought of quitting the country. He confessed that he had of late taken every opportunity of examining

W. H. G. Kingston

the new doctrines, and that he was acquainted enough with them to make him desire to go to England, where he might study them more freely, and with greater safety. "I know not what your opinions may be, Mr Hopper, but I am very sure that you will not mention mine to any one else."

The merchant was generally cautious, but the young man's apparent frankness threw him greatly off his guard. Caspar, urged on by Father Quixada, persevered, and at length fully persuaded the merchant Hopper that he was a convert to the Protestant faith. A private meeting of Protestants was to take place, and Caspar entreated that he might be allowed to be present. The merchant no longer hesitated. At the meeting prayers were offered up, hymns sung, and the simple Gospel plainly put before those present. The young man listened attentively in spite of himself. He there learned that all men are sinners and justly condemned; that "God so loved the world that He gave His only-begotten Son" to suffer instead of sinful man, and to save him from the result of that determination. He heard that "the just shall live by faith," not by any works, not by any good deeds that they can do, not by any forms and ceremonies to which they may adhere, but simply trusting to the blood shed for them on Calvary, to the perfect and complete sacrifice offered up by Christ for them. He there learned that Jesus Christ had become sinful man's sin-bearer; that He had fulfilled the obedience which man had neglected to fulfil; that He came to save sinners, to lift the weary and heart-broken, the wretched and the penitent, out of their miserable state; that man is saved simply by turning away from his sins, from his idolatries, from the thoughtless course he may have hitherto followed, and looking trustfully, believingly, on Jesus crucified for him. The young man went away from the meeting with new thoughts, but with an unchanged heart. He had promised to go immediately to Father Quixada, and he fulfilled his promise, though not without doubt and hesitation.

"You have done well," said the father. "Let me once get among these people, and I will put a stop to their preaching, while you may make sure of winning pretty Gretchen for your wife, and perchance come in for a share of the merchant's property, which I may secure for you."

There was to be another meeting the following night. Caspar passed the interval in a state of doubt and agitation. He had promised to introduce the father, who, disguised as a German merchant just arrived from the South, was eager to be present. Often the young man thought he would try and persuade the father not to go, then that he would positively refuse to introduce him. He had, however, already given him so much information that he would have had no difficulty in finding his way to the place of meeting by himself. Still, Caspar might acknowledge his own treacherous intentions and warn the Protestants of the spy who was about to be in their midst. The cunning priest soon discovered his perplexity, and used every argument to induce him to be satisfied that he was doing the right thing. Caspar was over-persuaded, but not convinced. The evening came, the meeting took place, and the German merchant was received as a Christian brother by those present. He noted them all, old men, young men, and women of various ranks.

Father Quixada heard the same truths which had been listened to by Caspar Gaill, but they fell on ground of a different character. He went away utterly regardless of them. He had now, not only the merchant Hopper, but several other influential and wealthy citizens in his power. He wished, however, to get more into his net, and hearing that in a day or two another meeting would take place, at which several other persons would attend, he laid his plans accordingly. "I shall have a good haul by that time," he thought to himself.

Caspar Gaill had in the meantime been seized with remorse.

He had betrayed the man who had trusted him, the father of one whom he wished to make his bride; still he dared not warn them. The friar, he well knew, had his eye upon him. He knew too completely the secrets of his heart, and he felt sure that should he attempt to defeat Father Quixada's projects, he himself would be the first victim of his vengeance.

At the intended meeting, not only the merchant Hopper, but his fair daughter Gretchen was present. Caspar Gaill came also, but how different were his thoughts to those he had entertained when first he entered that hall!

He kept looking anxiously round, hoping that the German merchant might not appear. His heart sank, however, when, just before the sermon began, the seeming merchant appeared, and was, to human eye, the most devout of all the congregation. No one joined more heartily in the hymns of Marot; no one seemed to hang more earnestly on the words of the speaker. Again were the glorious truths of the Gospel put forth in simple language. Though the merchant's eyes were fixed on the speaker, and his countenance beamed with intelligence, his thoughts were far away, occupied in a plan for capturing the whole of those who were engaged in worship round him. His quick eye, too, was noting all who were present. He marked the fair Gretchen, and knew her at once from being with her father.

"Caspar has not chosen ill, so far as eye is concerned," he said to himself. "No wonder he raves about the little maiden. He need no longer have any fears about winning her; she may not love him, but surely she will rather become his bride than be sent to the stake. Few girls would prefer burning, or drowning, or hanging, to a young and gallant husband. Caspar is well-favoured, she will not refuse him; we will give her the choice."

The meeting was brought to a conclusion. Father Quixada left the hall with the rest, and after making several turns and twists so as to escape observation, he took his way to the house where a newly-arrived bishop lodged, sent from Brussels to look into the religious condition of Brill. The bishop and Father Quixada were of kindred spirit. The former held an important office in the Holy Inquisition, and felt no compunction, but on the contrary, considerable satisfaction, at sending a dozen of his fellow-creatures to suffer death by drowning, or burning, because they might differ from him on a few theological points. Father Quixada explained the plan he had adopted, and received the warm approval of his superior.

It was late at night. The fair Gretchen was about to retire to her room. The merchant had been engaged at his books and accounts. He had been collecting such property as he could put into a portable form, and had made up his mind to leave Brill forthwith for England. He had communicated his intentions to Peter Kopplestock, who highly approved of them, and had engaged to put him on board a vessel the following morning by daybreak. There was a knock at the door. The merchant himself, attended by Barbara the housekeeper, went with a light to open it. A figure wrapped in a cloak was standing there.

"Admit me for a moment," said the stranger. "I come to warn you of danger."

He entered, and the light held by Barbara fell on the features of Caspar Gaill.

"I come to entreat you to fly immediately. Even now I may be too late. The officers of the Inquisition are already proceeding through the city, to capture certain suspected persons. You are among them. I dare not wait another moment; no mercy would be shown me if I was discovered."

The unhappy young man spoke in a low, trembling voice. Tears were in his eyes; he was pale as death.

Again he hastened forth. He had not dared to confess the whole truth. The merchant closed the door, and proceeded with yet greater speed with his preparations. He sent Barbara to Gretchen's room to tell her to prepare for flight. During the housekeeper's absence there was another knock at the door. It was repeated with far greater violence when those without found that it was not opened. After the warning he had received, the merchant guessed too well who were his visitors. He hastily concealed the property he was about to carry off, and the other articles he had prepared for his departure. He then sent Barbara to the door, who, with unwilling hands, began slowly to withdraw the bolts.

"What is the matter?" she asked; "what are you in such a hurry for? Why do you thus disturb quiet citizens from their early rest?"

So nervous was she, however, that she could scarcely continue her interrogations. At length the last bolt was withdrawn, and a party in dark cloaks and masks were seen at the door.

"Where are your master and his daughter?" asked one of them; "they must accompany us forthwith."

"My master and his daughter!" asked Barbara, "what can you want with them at this hour of the night?"

"They must come to the Holy Office, to answer certain questions," answered the speaker. "Lead the way."

"But if the door is opened the light will be blown out, and you will be unable to follow me."

Her great aim was to delay as long as possible, in the hope that by some means her master and Gretchen might make their escape by the back of the house. She was greatly in hope that the light would blow out, that she might thus have an excuse for a longer delay.

"Come—come! no fooling, mistress!" exclaimed the officer. "Lead on, or we must find the way by ourselves."

On this, Barbara proceeded up the broad steps to the floor above. Two or three men, however, kept watch below. In vain were all her precautions. In the usual sitting room, quietly seated at a table, were Gretchen and her father. They rose as the officers of the Inquisition entered, and the merchant asked them what they wanted. The officer repeated what he had said to Barbara.

"We must obey," said the merchant; "we have no power to resist."

Instantly the father and daughter were surrounded, and carried off separately. Poor Barbara wrung her hands in terror as she saw them depart. They were carried along to the prison in which those accused by the Inquisition were confined. Brill had for some time been free from such visitations, but the presence of Alva at Brussels had stirred up the authorities, and victims were sought for throughout every town in Flanders.

They were not allowed to languish long in prison before their trial took place. It was very short, for they did not deny the accusations brought against them. They refused to acknowledge that the elements of bread and wine were really the body and blood of Christ.

"Christ is in heaven," answered the merchant Hopper, "at the right hand of God; He cannot be on earth at the same time. I don't believe that sinful man, by a few words, would have the power of changing bread and wine into flesh and blood. If there was a change, our sense would give us evidence of that change. The bread remains bread, and the wine, wine. But more than this, I see no authority in Scripture for this belief. Christ told us to take bread and wine in remembrance of the last supper He took with His disciples on earth, or rather, of the great sacrifice which He was about to offer up, the last, the only one which God would ever accept, all previous ones being types of this; promising us the same support to our spiritual nature that the bread and wine gives to our physical nature. He often speaks of Himself as a door, as a rock, as a corner-stone of a building. In the same way He speaks of His flesh and blood. He intends us to understand that we are spiritually to feed on Him, that is to say, to trust on His sacrifice, His blood shed for us."

"This is heresy! You need say no more," said the judge. "And your daughter there, what does she say to these things?"

"I agree with my father," answered Gretchen, firmly. "I believe that the just shall live by faith; that neither our works nor our obedience to the Church of Rome will help in any way to save us. Christ has accomplished that great and glorious work, and only requires us to take hold of it by faith."

"Enough—enough!" exclaimed the Inquisitor, stamping; "you have condemned yourself by your own words. We need no other witnesses, though we can prove that you and others were present at heretical meetings. That circumstance alone was sufficient to condemn you to death. We may afford you a few days for consideration and repentance. If you will recant your errors, you may receive a more merciful sentence, but if not, you, Andrew Hopper, are condemned to be burned alive; and you, Gretchen Hopper, to be drowned in a tank at the place of execution."

Several other persons were brought up before the Inquisitors, the greater number of whom were condemned to death. Andrew Hopper's property was confiscated to the use of the state, or in other words, to assist Duke Alva in riveting yet more firmly his yoke upon the necks of their countrymen. Both Andrew Hopper and Gretchen Hopper bore their fate with firmness and resignation. The chief regret of his daughter was that she was separated from her father. She longed to be with him that she might comfort and support him. Her thoughts, too, occasionally went back to her lover Diedrich. Where was he all the time? Alas! she would never see him again in this world, but she prayed that he might remain firm to the truth, and meet her in a more glorious state of existence.

When Caspar Gaill found what had taken place, he was in despair. He felt inclined to throw himself into the Meuse, and there end his life. He accused himself, very justly, of having caused the destruction of one he professed to love.

Might he yet do anything to save Gretchen? She might, perhaps, be got off, though it was not likely that her father would be allowed to escape. At first he thought of trying to get Father Quixada to plead for Gretchen, but he shuddered when he remembered the character of the man, and felt that even should the priest get her off, her condition would possibly not be improved. At last he bethought himself of consulting Peter Kopplestock. He had already told him of his love for Gretchen, he might possibly induce the ferryman to assist in her escape—no easy task, however, and one full of perils. Peter had not before heard of the seizure of the merchant Hopper and his daughter. He was naturally indignant in the extreme against all concerned.

"We must be cautious, however," he said at length, recovering his calmness. "I tell you, however, Caspar Gaill, I believe you have had something to do with it. You may be sorry now when it is too late. However, you must now exert yourself. Your father and the Bishop of Mons are old friends. You must endeavour to get the execution of these people deferred for a few days. That will give me more time to devise a scheme for their escape. A little bribery will probably have considerable effect. You have plenty of wealth, expend it liberally in this cause; you may thus somewhat repair the harm you have done."

Caspar promised to follow the advice of Peter, declaring that he would spend every guilder he possessed to aid his object. Day after day passed by, the accused refused to recant, and the Inquisitor declared that he could not "longer delay affording the true Catholics in the place the pleasure of seeing their Protestant fellow-citizens committed to the flames."

Caspar bribed liberally as he promised, but though his money was taken there was no good result. At length the day arrived when the executions were to take place. A stage was erected with a gibbet on it and huge casks of water. Below, on the solid ground, stakes with chains were driven into the ground; while near the gibbet was a post with a chain in which those who were to be mercifully strangled before being thrown into the flames were to be placed. It was a fearful-looking spectacle— fearful from its very simplicity. There was no parade nor decoration, nothing to conceal the naked horror of the work.

CHAPTER FOUR

THE BEGGARS OF THE SEA—PETER CHERISHES
NEW HOPES—PETER IS SENT AS AN ENVOY
FROM THE ROVERS—THE EXECUTIONS ARE
SUSPENDED, AND CASPAR SENT TO TREAT WITH
THE BEGGARS—CASPAR RESIGNS GRETCHEN
TO DIEDRICH—THE BEGGARS OF THE SEA
ATTACK BRILL—DIEDRICH VISITS THE
INQUISITION—FATHER QUIXADA ATTEMPTS TO
KEEP HIS PRISONERS, BUT IS DEFEATED—BRILL
IS CAPTURED BY THE PROTESTANTS—AND
BECOMES THE CRADLE OF THE DUTCH
REPUBLIC

Peter Kopplestock was in despair. He had in vain attempted to obtain an interview with his young niece, or to send her any message. The prisoners were so strictly watched that he was unable even to send her a message. Her death and that of her worthy father seemed sealed. Peter in despair returned to his post; it was time for him to be ready to ferry passengers across the river. He had taken one party across, and was returning once more to Brill, when down the river a fleet of several large vessels was seen standing up towards the town. Peter watched them with interest. That they were not merchant vessels, he was well aware. They were not Spanish ships either. He came to the conclusion, therefore, that they

W. H. G. Kingston

must be the Beggars of the Sea. Concealing his own feelings, he informed his passengers, who wished to know his opinions. They were the powerful fleet of those redoubted rovers, and there could be little doubt that they had come up to attack Brill. By the time he had fully worked upon the fears of his passengers, they arrived at the landing-place on the side of the city. Instantly the whole party rushed up towards the town, spreading the alarming information they had received. He told them also that for their sakes he would venture down the river, and try and ascertain more particulars. Some urged him not to run so great a risk. He laughingly answered that it mattered little, that they could but hang him if he was caught, and that many an honest man was every day suffering a worse fate than that, thanks to the Duke of Alva.

Peter rowed away down the river as hard as he could urge on his boat. As he approached the fleet he was more convinced than ever that he was right. The first vessel he hailed was commanded, he was told, by William de Blois, Seigneur of Treslong, a noble whose brother had been executed by the Duke of Alva, and who had himself fought by the side of Count Louis at Yemmingen, where he was desperately wounded.

Kopplestock was an old acquaintance of his, and was immediately recognised. Treslong welcomed him warmly; he was the very man he wished to meet. Peter, nothing loth, communicated at once the events going forward in the city, and urged an immediate attack. Here was a means, he hoped, of saving his friends.

"Depend upon it we are not anxious to delay, for the honest truth is, we have scarcely a piece of biscuit or a lump of cheese remaining on board any of the ships in the fleet. Our fellows are literally starving, and land we must, somewhere or other, and forage for food. However, come, my friend, we will go on board the admiral's ship, and hear what he says to the proposal of an immediate attack."

Treslong, getting into Peter's boat, proceeded forthwith to the ship of Admiral De la Marck. The first person Peter caught sight of on board was Diedrich Megheni. Even Peter thought he had never seen a wilder set of ruffians than the crew of the flag-ship, but they were all far surpassed by the admiral himself. His hair was long and shaggy, his beard hung down over his chest, joined by his whiskers, pendant from his cheeks, while his huge moustache projected out far on either side. He was in no ways loth to attack the place. "My jolly Beggars will soon make themselves masters of the town," he observed; "but as you wish it, Treslong, we will see what diplomacy will do first. Who will take a message to the magistrates of the city?"

"Our worthy friend Peter Kopplestock will do so," observed Treslong. "Here, take my ring; it will accredit you as our envoy. If the town will surrender, we promise to treat all the inhabitants with consideration and tenderness; if not, they must take the consequences."

Peter, receiving further directions, jumped into his boat, and hurried back towards the town.

The hour for the execution of the condemned heretics was approaching. If he could work upon the fears of the Inquisitor, they might yet be saved.

While Peter is rowing with all his might up towards Brill, the sudden appearance of the ships of the Sea-beggars must be accounted for. The fleet of De la Marck had been lying for some time in different ports in the south of England, sallying forth occasionally and making prizes of Spanish ships. It was the policy of Queen Elizabeth and her Government at this time to remain at peace; and the Duke of Alva's commissioners had been urging on her that the continued countenance afforded by the English to the Beggars of the Sea must inevitably lead to a war with Spain. Towards the end of March, therefore, De la Marck received a peremptory order from Elizabeth to quit the shores of England, while her subjects were forbidden to supply them with meat, bread, beer, or any other necessaries. The rover fleet set sail, therefore, from Dover, on one of the last days in March, with scarcely any provisions on board. They stood over, accordingly, towards the coast of Zealand; and finally entered, as has been described, the river Meuse.

Peter quickly reached the town, and pushed through the crowd of inhabitants, who came round him, asking him all sorts of questions, to none of which he would reply, except to say that a large force of the Water-beggars, some thousands, as far as he could tell, were about to enter the city, and cut all their throats if they were opposed, or if they found that any of their friends had been injured.

"Take care what the Inquisitors are about," he added. "If these people whom they have condemned to death are executed, depend upon it the Water-beggars will put every man and woman in the place to death. Just see about that matter."

Pushing on, he made his appearance in the town-house, where the magistrates were assembled. He told them that he had been sent by the fierce Admiral De la Marck, and by Treslong, who was well known to them; that two commissioners on the part of the city should be sent out to confer with them. He had to assure them that the deputies would be courteously treated, and he was ordered to say that the only object of those who had sent him was to free the land, and to overthrow the tyranny of the Spaniards.

"And how many men under him has De la Marck, do you think?" asked the chief magistrate.

"It would be difficult for me to count them," answered Peter, carelessly, "considering I only saw some of their ships; but there are probably some five thousand in all, more or less; but they are desperate fellows, and equal to twice the number of ordinary mortals."

On hearing this, the magistrates made long faces at each other.

"It is clear that we cannot resist such a force," observed one; "but what shall we do? Shall we negotiate, or shall we fly?"

"In my opinion, it would be judicious to do both," observed a sagacious old burgher. "We should negotiate in order to gain time to run away."

"But which two men will be found to proceed to the rebel fleet as our envoys?" asked another. "It is an honourable post, is no one ready to fill it?"

There seemed a great likelihood of the negotiations breaking down for want of envoys to carry them on. At this juncture Caspar Gaill made his appearance in the court-house.

"I will go," he said, "on one condition: that the executions which were to take place this morning are suspended. If we put to death the fellow-religionists of these people, they are not likely to treat us with much mercy."

The justice of Caspar's remark was at once seen; and in spite of the protestations of the Inquisitor and the other priests, that it would be impious to take their victims out of the hands of the Church, the magistracy decided that the criminals should be immediately respited.

"If we determine on fighting, and put the enemy to flight, you holy fathers may then execute due punishment on the heretics," observed one of the magistrates; "but, in the meantime, we prefer not to subject ourselves to the rage of these desperate freebooters."

Caspar quickly persuaded another friend to accompany him on board the fleet, and, rowed by Peter, they proceeded on board the admiral's ship. It was there the rivals met. Caspar, before entering the admiral's cabin, had just time to exchange a few words with Diedrich.

"I resign Gretchen to you," he whispered; "I am not worthy of her. I acted a vile and treacherous part, and was very nearly the cause of the destruction of her and her father. They are now, I trust, safe; unless those vile priests prove treacherous. At all events there is no time to be lost in hastening on shore, that they may be completely rescued from their power."

As soon as the message of the magistrates was received, the sailors quickly leaped into their boats, and hastened on shore. The rovers were divided into two parties. One, under Treslong, made an attack upon the southern gates; while the other, commanded by the admiral, advanced upon the northern. The governor of the city, it appeared, had not agreed to the proposals of the magistrates, and had made preparations to resist their entrance. Hungry men, especially of the character of the sea-rovers, are not likely to be stopped by trifles. Treslong and his followers forthwith attacked the gates with great fury. Just at the moment that they forced an entrance, the governor of the city was endeavouring to take his departure. He was, however, arrested by the rovers. Meantime De la Marck and his men, lighting a huge fire at the northern gate, rigged a battering-ram, formed out of a ship's mast; and as the fire burned the wood of the gates, they commenced battering away with might and main. The gates quickly gave way; and, dashing the embers of the fire aside, the bold sailors, sword in hand, rushed into the town, and speedily found themselves masters of the place. Among those who had accompanied Treslong was Diedrich Meghem. Peter Kopplestock had kept by his side. A choice band of seamen had followed Diedrich.

"Follow me, lads," he exclaimed, as soon as they were inside the gates; "our first work must be to set the prisoners of the Inquisition free."

He and Peter rushed on, followed by a party of seamen. The Inquisitors and monks endeavoured to prevent their entrance. The doors were very soon battered in. Gretchen, who expected every instant to be led forth to execution, was on her knees in her cell. She heard the noise, little suspecting the cause. At that moment the door opened, and a monk appeared. She looked up, and beheld the stern features of Father Quixada. There was a glance in his eye which made her tremble.

"Have you come to lead me to death?" she asked.

"No, I would give you your liberty; follow me."

"No; I will not," she exclaimed, regarding him with a look of horror.

He rushed forward, and seized her by the arm, and was dragging her along the passage, when footsteps were heard approaching; and the ray of sunlight which streamed along

W. H. G. Kingston

the passage fell on a party of men who were hurrying through it. Their leader was Diedrich Meghem. With a cry of joy, Gretchen, tearing herself from the grasp of the monk, darted forward towards another part of the prison. The patriot seamen soon discovered the cell in which the merchant Hopper was confined, and he and all the other prisoners were quickly liberated. A large number of the citizens had escaped; but several monks and priests who had remained in the convent were captured, as well as the governor and some other civil authorities. Admiral De la Marck took possession of the town in the name of the Prince of Orange. Thus the weary spirit of freedom, so long a fugitive over earth and sea, at length found a resting-place; and the foundation of the Dutch Republic was laid in the little city of Brill. No indignity was offered to the inhabitants of either sex, and all those who remained were treated with consideration. The captors, however, took possession of the best houses, and very naturally made themselves at home. The inclination to plunder the churches, however, could not long be restrained. The altars and images were destroyed, while the rich furniture and the gorgeous vestments of the priests were appropriated by the rovers. Adam van Haren, who commanded one of the ships, appeared on his vessel's deck attired in a magnificent high-mass chasuble; while his seamen dressed themselves up in the various other vestments which the Romish clergy had been wont to wear on their grand festivals. So great was the hatred of the admiral for everything connected with the Church of Rome, that thirteen unfortunate monks and priests, including Father Quixada, who had been taken prisoners, were, by his orders, a few days after the capture of the city, executed in the very way that they had intended to put to death the victims of the Inquisition. Caspar Gaill joined the fleet of De la Marck, and was soon afterwards killed in an action with some Spanish ships. In spite of Duke Alva's attempt to retake Brill, the city remained ever afterwards faithful to the Prince of Orange.

Diedrich and Gretchen were the first persons united according to the Protestant form in Brill, after its capture, and their descendants have ever been among its most respected inhabitants.

CHAPTER FIVE

FRANK CARLTON—A STORY OF NIAGARA

NIAGARA—ITS GRANDEUR AND DANGERS—
FANNY REJECTS FRANK BECAUSE HE IS NOT A
HERO—SCARCITY OF HEROES—FANNY'S
NEPHEWS GET INTO A BOAT—THEY DRIFT
AWAY—NO HOPE—HELP AT THE LAST—A
FEARFUL STRUGGLE—FANNY FINDS FRANK IS A
HERO AFTER ALL

Niagara, the father of waters! The name is significant of something grand; words are inadequate to describe the mighty cataract. The waters which rush down from Lake Superior, passing through Lake Huron and Lake Saint Clair, and onward across Lake Erie, finally force their course in a northern direction into Lake Ontario. On first leaving Lake Erie, they flow in a tranquil current, and divide, leaving an island in the centre, on which a thousand cattle save one are said to feed. Then the rapidity of the current increases, till those who voyage on its bosom see in front of them, raised high in the blue sky, a cloud of vapour. This is said to be the crown of Niagara, the vapoury particles collecting from the boiling caldron below.

Proceeding onward, a roaring sound is heard, the current

increases in rapidity, and ahead appears a line of foaming breakers. Those who once get within their power must give up all hope of life. No vessel built with mortal hands can live amidst those furious rapids. In the centre a rocky island appears, thickly covered with trees, and while one portion of the stream rushes directly on, and takes a leap downwards of 200 feet, the other and smaller portion, sweeping round Goat Island, finds its way into the lower level, over the cliff on the right bank of the river. The last-mentioned fall is known as the American fall, as the territory on that side of the river belongs to the United States.

Onward the waters rush, between lofty cliffs, at a distance of three miles, when they meet an opposing rock, and, circling round and round, form a fearful whirlpool. No one falling into that circling eddy has ever escaped with life. The stoutest boat would soon be dashed to pieces.

At length the waters find their way out by a narrow passage, and rush onward into Lake Ontario. A long fall across the direct current of the River is known as the Horseshoe Fall. Standing on the British bank of the stream, it is seen on the right, with the American fall directly opposite the spectator. In the latter fall many fearful accidents have occurred.

The scenery above the Falls is very different to that below. In the latter the banks are high and precipitous, and the stream flows on 200 feet below the summit of the cliffs. Above the cataract, on the contrary, the river presents the appearance rather of a large lake. The woods, consisting of firs, and birch, and maple, come close down to the water, their branches overhanging the stream. Here and there are clearings. Many mills moved by water power, and numerous farms, extend along the banks on either side.

It was somewhere above the rapids that a young man, clad in

homely costume but with the appearance and bearing of a gentleman, was walking by the river's brink. By his side was a fair girl. He was speaking to her earnestly and gently, but she seemed to be turning an indifferent ear to his words.

"I acknowledge your merits, Mr Carlton, but really I cannot see that I should be expected to give my heart and hand, as you ask me, to one who has not done anything to show that he is above the ordinary run of respectable young gentlemen." The girl spoke in a somewhat bantering tone.

"But really, Miss Fanny Aveling, you are expecting too much at the present day. Gentlemen cannot go forth with a lance and fight in tournaments, as in days of yore, to win the admiration of the ladies of their love. I offer you an honest heart, and I have every reason to believe I shall establish a comfortable home; and really I think that is a more sensible thing than running the risk of getting a knock on the head for no purpose whatever."

"How fearfully matter-of-fact you are," answered Fanny. "I tell you I do not like matter-of-fact people. If you had been a soldier or sailor, and had fought the battles of your country, and got wounded, and obtained a number of medals for your gallantry, I might possibly have felt differently towards you."

"But I have had no opportunity of doing anything of the sort," urged Frank Carlton. "I came out here to form an estate, and I have succeeded in what I undertook, while a number of other persons with similar opportunities have failed. I do not say this for the sake of boasting, but simply as a fact which is certainly not discreditable."

"Humdrum," answered the young lady, half to herself. "Numbers have done as well."

"So they have," said Frank Carlton, "and are married and settled, and have every reason to be thankful that they came to the country."

"Well, Mr Carlton, there is no use carrying on the conversation further," exclaimed Fanny: "You ask me to give you my heart and hand; I frankly confess I have no inclination to do so."

"But, surely, you have led me to suppose you would," said Frank, in a tone of reproach.

"That was when I did not think you in earnest," said Fanny. "If you had said this before, I should have given you an answer which might then have satisfied you."

"Nothing will satisfy me but 'yes,'" said Frank, "for I believe that you have more sense than you pretend to have."

"That is to say, you think I have sense enough to love you," said Fanny, still in a tone of banter. "We part as friends, however, and if you insist on coming to call upon my sister, Mrs Barton, of course I cannot help it, only do not for a moment suppose that I give you any encouragement."

Frank Carlton, having graduated at Oxford, had come out a few years before to set up as a farmer in Canada. He had enjoyed the advantage of studying under a Scotch farmer for a year, and this gave him more knowledge of agricultural affairs than is possessed by many of the young men who go out to settle. He had also given his mind to the work, and what was of great importance, had withstood the temptations to idleness into which so many fall. He was also a man of refined tastes and habits, which he did not allow the rough life of a settler to make him abandon. Captain and Mrs Barton were among his nearest neighbours. He had been for

W. H. G. Kingston

some time a constant visitor at the house, and two little boys, the children of Mrs Barton, were his especial favourites.

Fanny Aveling had, the year before, come out from England, and not long after her arrival Frank Carlton began to reflect that his house would be in a far better condition than it was at the present, if he could place a mistress at its head. He had had no reason to suppose that Miss Aveling was indifferent towards him, until the day on which the conversation which has been described took place. He was still, it must be owned, somewhat in doubt about the matter. He did not suppose that she cared for anybody else; indeed he knew of no visitor at the house likely to have won her affections. He therefore, as most men would have done under similar circumstances, lived on in the hope of ultimately winning her. Still, week after week passed, and though he made frequent visits to Captain Barton's, Miss Aveling's manner towards him remained totally unchanged. At length, sanguine as he was, he began to fear that he had misplaced his affections. He also grew distant in his manner towards her, and he seldom paid a visit to the house of his former friends.

Mrs Barton could not but suspect the cause, for she, it must be owned, was favourable to Frank Carlton, and thought that her sister could not make a more desirable match.

"What more can you require in a man than Frank possesses, Fanny?" she said one day to her sister.

"Yes," observed Fanny, "he is honest, and he does not smoke, and he does not drink, and he does not use bad language, that I know of, and he's very respectable; in fact, in my opinion, he is made up of negatives."

"Oh, you foolish girl!" exclaimed Mrs Barton; "you want

him to threaten to leave you for ever, or to jump down the Falls, or to commit some other outrageous act, and then perhaps your feelings would be worked up, and you would be ready to entreat him to remain and be yours."

"No, I tell you I don't care for him, that I know of, and don't know that I ever shall," answered Fanny, petulantly. "I have made up my mind, when he next comes, to let him understand that very clearly."

As it happened, Frank paid another visit the following day to the Bartons. Fanny certainly did contrive to show him that there were no hopes of her becoming his wife.

He would make a tour through the country, visit Toronto, Montreal, and perhaps go down to Quebec. Or he would make a trip to the Far West, across Lake Superior to the Red River Settlement, and visit the small band of his countrymen collected there. At first he thought he would start at once, and not pay a farewell visit to the Bartons.

It happened that Mrs Barton, her sister, and her two little boys, Frank's favourites, Ernest and Harry, were strolling about by the bank of the river. They had gone somewhere down in the direction of the rapids, when Fanny exclaimed that the scenery, already tinged by the bright hue of autumn, was so beautiful that she must stop and make a sketch.

The two sisters sat down on the bank, while Fanny, with the hand of an artist, rapidly sketched the scene. She had to employ the most gorgeous colours which her colour-box could supply, and even then could scarcely give sufficient brightness to the landscape. While she was sketching, the little boys ran along the bank, where, moored to the shore, they found a boat, and very naturally got into it. Their mother and aunt did not observe them. They got out the oars, and began to make believe that they were rowing. Now they pulled on one side and then on the other. Harry, the youngest, tired of rowing, put in the oar, and began to play with the "painter." The boat had been carelessly secured, and by some means or other he let the painter slip. Ernest, in the meantime, who was still rowing, turned the boat round, and before the boys knew what was happening, they were drifting from the shore. Already, before they saw their danger, they were too far off to regain the bank. Often they had been told of the fearful risk of being carried off by the current. They screamed with fear. Their cries aroused their mother and aunt. Several people also had been attracted by them from a neighbouring farm, but no boat was to be seen at hand in which they could be followed. Already the boat was moving down the current. It was still some distance from the rapids: but, unless stopped in its course, it must eventually reach them.

Mrs Barton and Fanny cried in vain to the spectators to aid in rescuing the children. Some of the men ran along the bank up the stream, but others stood still, and declared they had no power to save the children.

"Still, if you would but swim in, you might get on board the boat before it has gone far," exclaimed Mrs Barton.

"And run a pretty fair chance of losing our own lives," was the reply made by some of the men.

Some way down, another boat was at length seen. It was a small, frail skiff, and moored very near the commencement of the rapids.

"Will any one try and save my children?" exclaimed Mrs Barton in despair.

Again the men shook their heads.

"Not for a thousand pounds. Before one could reach the boat in that rotten canoe, she would be among the rapids."

The fond mother and Fanny became almost frantic with despair. Just at that moment a figure was seen bounding down from a neighbouring height. In an instant, with a knife, he cut the painter securing the skiff to the shore. A pair of paddles were in the skiff. He leaped in and shoved off from the bank. Mrs Barton knew him, and so did Fanny.

"It's Frank Carlton!" they exclaimed. "Oh, blessings on him! May God protect him!"

Already the boat was approaching the commencement of the rapids. Once in their power, even his sturdy arms could scarcely stem the current. Not for one moment did he calculate the difficulty or danger he was to undergo. With rapid strokes he pursued the floating boat. How eagerly did the fond mother watch his proceedings! She stood apparently calm on the bank, only now and then extending her arms, as if she would draw back the boat which contained her loved ones.

Still, to those who looked on it seemed scarcely possible that the children could escape. If they were lost, so also would be Frank Carlton. Still he pursued. The motion of the boat which contained the boys showed its near approach to the rapids. In two or three minutes it would be within their power. It seemed hardly credible that he could reach it even in that time. Onward he went, every now and then turning his head round to watch the boat. Already it began to leap and toss. The water foamed around it.

"See! he has got alongside!" exclaimed the people from the

W. H. G. Kingston

shore; "but will he have strength to stem the current on his return?"

A glance showed him that two oars were in the boat. Leaving his canoe to its fate, he leaped into the boat, and seized the oars. Now came a fearful struggle. Should an oar give way, he and his young friends must inevitably be lost. He nerved himself for the undertaking by offering up prayer for strength to One who alone can give it. Grasping the oars, he placed his feet firmly at the bottom of the boat, and rowed manfully. At first it seemed to those who looked on that he made no way. The boat's head was up the stream, but still she seemed to be going slowly and surely downwards. He struggles on. The water foams around the boat on every side. Yes! he is making way—he has gained an inch, another and another. Slowly the boat moves onward, out of the power of the rapids. A foot is gained. Still, by the exertions he is making, his strength must become exhausted. He rows on and on; the boat makes headway. Surely the prayers of that fond mother are heard. The gallant young man renews his exertions. He is resolved, God helping him, to save the children. He thinks not of himself, or what will be the consequences to his own frame. The veins seem starting from his forehead. Those only who have gone through such a contest, can understand what he had to endure. The people from the neighbouring farms now eagerly crowd the shores, ready to render him assistance when he reaches it. Some, however, even now doubt whether he will accomplish the undertaking. Should his strength fail, even for an instant, the boat would quickly be carried back, with those on board, to destruction. With all his strength he continues rowing, looking neither to the right hand nor the left. His eyes are on the young children who sit crouching down in terror at the bottom of the boat. With a smile, he endeavours to encourage them. Again and again he cries to Heaven for strength. Gradually the boat approaches the shore. Now it has reached an upward eddy. Still he rows on, and the boat safely reaches the bank. Scarcely conscious of his success, he is lifted out of the boat, and eager hands restore the children to their mother. She clasps them to her bosom, and pours out her gratitude to their deliverer. But there is one kneeling by his side who entreats those who stand by to bring some water to bathe his brow. The handkerchief tied round his throat is loosened. He returns to consciousness, and sees Fanny Aveling bending over him. In a short time he declares himself sufficiently recovered to walk, and a joyful party returned to Barton Lodge.

Our tale is finished. Though he returned home that evening, Frank could not do otherwise than, the following morning, visit Barton Lodge, to enquire after the boys. Fanny Aveling no longer received him as had been her wont.

"You have done something," she exclaimed. "Yes, I see it is not necessary for a man to go and fight, and kill his fellow-creatures, to be a hero. Oh, Frank, what a very silly girl I have been!"

Frank assured her he was confident she would be a wise woman in future, and it is scarcely necessary to add that Frank's establishment soon had a mistress at its head.

CHAPTER SIX

FAITHFUL AND BRAVE

A BIG SCAMP AND A TRUE MAN—ELLIS VISITED
BY HIS SWEETHEART—READS HIS BIBLE ON
BOARD SHIP—TRIALS AND PERSECUTIONS—
ELLIS KNOCKS JONES DOWN— DANGER—JONES
SHIRKS AND ELLIS ENCOUNTERS IT—A
CHRISTIAN WOMAN'S TEST— A TERRIBLE
PREDICAMENT—THE MIDDY SAVED BY ELLIS—
AND THE SAILORS ASCRIBE IT TO THE POWER
OF PRAYER

I was many years ago, first-lieutenant of the *Rainbow* frigate. We were fitting out alongside the old *Topaz* hulk, in Portsmouth Harbour, for the North American and West India stations, at that time united under one command. We were nearly ready for sea, but still were a good many hands short of our complement. For want of better, we had entered several men, who would, I was afraid, prove but hard bargains; one especially, who gave the name of John Jones, was a great, big, hulking fellow, with an unpleasant expression of countenance, out of whom I guessed but little work was to be got. The same day he joined, another man came aboard and volunteered. He was a fine, active, intelligent fellow. He said that his name was William Ellis, and that he had been eight years at sea, in the merchant service. If there was little work in Jones, there was plenty in him I saw, though he was a remarkably quiet-looking man. He answered the questions put to him, but did not volunteer a word about himself.

We had gone out to Spithead, and the Blue Peter was flying aloft, when a shore boat came alongside. In the boat was a young woman, nicely, though very plainly dressed, and a lad, who looked like her brother. She asked leave to come on board, and inquired for William Ellis. Ellis was aloft. His name had been loudly called along the lower deck, before, casting his eyes below, having finished his work, they fell on her. She gave a half-shriek of terror as she saw him, quick as lightning, gliding down the rigging. He, in another moment, was by her side. A blush was on his manly cheek, as he took her hand and warmly pressed it. They talked earnestly for some time. He did not ask her to move from the spot where they stood. At length, with a sigh, having shaken hands with the lad, he prepared to help her into the boat. Her last words, pronounced in a firm, though sweet voice, were, "Oh! remember."

I was particularly struck by her quiet, modest manner, and her pleasing, intelligent expression of countenance. We had despatches for Jamaica and other West India Islands, which we visited in turn. Ellis continued, as at first, one of the most quiet, well-behaved men in the ship. Every moment of his watch below—that is to say, when off duty— he was engaged in reading, chiefly, as I afterwards found, the Bible. In those days, a Bible on the lower deck was a rarity, and religious books were still less often seen. The *Rainbow* formed no exception to the rule, and Ellis got to be looked at with suspicion and dislike by the greater number of the men. He was equally disliked by some of the officers. The reason was clear—his life and example was a reproach to them.

W. H. G. Kingston

We had not been long in that treacherous clime before "Yellow Jack," as sailors call the yellow fever, came on board. Numbers of our crew were speedily down with it. Several died, and the pestilence increased. The ship's company, as sometimes occurs, took a panic, and men who would boldly have faced a visible enemy, trembled with dread at the thoughts of being struck down by the fever. It was difficult to get men to attend properly on the sick. Ellis was an exception; he immediately volunteered for that duty, and was indefatigable in its performance. He did more, I found; he spoke words of counsel and encouragement to the sick and dying; he pointed out to them the Saviour, on whom looking with repentance and faith in His all-sufficient work, they might be assured of forgiveness.

Harry Lethbridge, a young midshipman, was among the first attacked. Ellis carefully watched over the boy. Whenever he had performed his other duties, he returned to the side of the hammock in which Harry lay, bathed his face, sponged out his mouth, and gave him cooling drinks, like the most gentle of nurses. More than once the doctor told me, however, that he was afraid the young midshipman would slip through his fingers, and he afterwards said that he considered it was mostly owing to the very great attention paid to him by Ellis that he had escaped. Ellis did more; he spoke to Harry, when his strength was returning, in a way to touch his heart,—he told him how he had been saved from the jaws of death by a God who loved his soul, and he showed how alone that soul could be saved, and how freely and fully it would be saved, if he would but accept the redemption offered him.

Notwithstanding the way Ellis had behaved during the fever, John Jones, and men of his stamp, of whom there were many, continued to sneer at him on account of his religion. "Any old woman, or young girl, could have done as well as he did,—nursing a few sick men and boys: what was that!"

they said. "It didn't make him a bit more of a man."

From the West Indies we were sent to North America, to do away with the effects of the fever. Knowing what a quiet man Ellis was, I was somewhat surprised when one day, on the passage to Halifax, John Jones came up to me on deck, fuming with rage, and preferred a formal charge against him, for having assaulted and thrashed him. I, of course, as in duty bound, sent for Ellis, and witnesses on both sides, to examine into the case. Ellis appeared, hat in hand, and at once acknowledged that he had thrashed Jones, but offered as an excuse that Jones and other men had systematically annoyed him whenever he sat down to read the Bible, and that at last Jones, encouraged by his previous forbearance, had snatched up the book and made off with it, threatening to throw it overboard. "I could bear it no longer, sir," said Ellis; "so I knocked him over, that I might get back my Bible, and read it afterwards in peace. Besides, sir, he said that people who read the Bible are never worth anything, only just fit to nurse sick people, and that come a gale of wind, or any danger, they would always be found skulking below."

"In that respect you, Jones, are wrong, and you had no business to snatch away Ellis's Bible; but you, Ellis, broke through the rules of discipline by knocking Jones over. You must reserve your blows for the enemies of your country. I must therefore punish you. It is your first offence, but it is too serious a one to be overlooked. Go below."

I inflicted as light a punishment as I well could on Ellis. After he had undergone it, he came to me and expressed his regret at having lost his temper, without in any way attempting to exculpate himself.

We reached Halifax, remained there a fortnight refitting, and again sailed to cruise off the coast. Nova Scotia possesses a

W. H. G. Kingston

rocky, forbidding shore, near which a seaman would dislike to be caught with a gale blowing on it. One night, on a passage round to Prince Edward's Island, we had kept closer in shore, in consequence of the fineness of the weather, than would, under other circumstances, have been prudent. The captain was ill below. Suddenly the wind shifted, and blew directly on shore. I was called up, and hurrying on deck, saw at once that we were to have a rough night of it.

The first thing to be done was to get a good offing. Accordingly I hauled to the wind, and as it was not yet blowing very hard, I kept the canvas on her which had previously been set. Suddenly a squall, its approach unseen, struck the ship, and before a sheet could be started, the main-topgallant yard was carried away, and the spar, wildly beating about in the now furiously-blowing gale, threatened to carry away, not only the topgallant mast, but the topmast itself. The loss of more of our spars at such a moment might have been disastrous in the extreme. To clear away the spar was, therefore of the greatest importance, but it was an operation which would expose those who attempted it to the most imminent dangers.

I sung out for volunteers. At that moment seeing Jones standing near me, I could not help saying, "Come, my man, there's work for you; you were boasting of your manhood the other day!" The first to spring forward to my call was William Ellis.

"No," I answered; "I have made the offer to Jones. He ought to succeed if any man can."

Jones looked aloft, then shook his head.

"I dare not; the man who attempts it will be sure to lose his life."

Ellis, as if anticipating the reply Jones would make, had been securing an axe to his belt; having felt the edge to assure himself that it was sharp. Scarcely had Jones finished speaking, than, exclaiming, "I'll go!" he was ascending the main rigging.

I watched him with intense anxiety as long as I could see him, but he was soon lost to sight in the gloom of night up aloft there amid the tightening ropes, the straining mast, and the loosened sail and shattered spar, which kept driving backwards and forwards and round and round with terrific violence. I kept my eyes fixed on the spot where I knew he must be. Now I thought I saw him clinging on to the rigging with one hand, while with the other, his axe gleaming above his head, he made stroke after stroke at the ropes by which the topgallant yard still hung to the mast. Had he been hurled from the rigging, the ocean would have been his tomb, for, heeling over as the ship was, he would have fallen far to leeward. I fully expected such would be his fate; it might be mine too, for I was determined to make the attempt if others failed. I thought of the young woman who had visited him on board, and of her sorrowing heart. My eye caught sight of something falling. Was it Ellis? No! A shout rose from the crew. Down came the shattered spar and the torn sail clear of everything, and fell into the foaming, hissing waters, through which the frigate was forcing her way. The topgallant mast stood uninjured. Ellis the next minute was beside me on the deck.

"Thank you, Ellis; you did that work nobly," I said to him. "I think that no one in future will venture to taunt you for your Bible-reading propensities."

I was now able to send the hands aloft to shorten sail, and I fully believe that our masts, and the ship herself, and our lives, were saved by that act of courage. I afterwards asked

Ellis how he felt when aloft.

"That I was in the hands of God, sir," he answered. "I prayed for His protection, and I never felt my heart more light, or my courage more firm." [See Note.]

As may be supposed, no one after this ventured to call Ellis a milksop, or to speak disparagingly of him in any other way. Jones sunk in public estimation as Ellis rose, and gained great influence among the ship's company, which he did not fail to use to their benefit. He still further increased it by another act, which, however, was not so much a proof of courage as of presence of mind, only the sailors declared, with a tinge of superstition, that no other man on board could have done it. I will mention it presently.

I frequently spoke to Ellis in a way an officer cannot venture to do, except to a well-tried man. One day I asked him if he did not wish to write to his wife, as I had the opportunity of sending letters.

"I am not married, sir," he answered, calmly. "That young woman you saw, sir, Mary Summers, has promised to marry me when I get back, if I can prove to her that I have acted all the time I have been away like a Christian man. It's a long story too, and I won't trouble you with it now; only Mary has very strong notions, and very right notions too. I wasn't once what I now try to be. I was altogether careless about religion. I fell in love with Mary, and tried my best to appear good, and so far succeeded that I won her love. When, however, she found out what I really was she said that nothing would induce her to marry me unless I was a Christian. She gave me books and I read them, and I read the Bible as I had never read it before, and she talked to me till I thought that I was what she wanted me to be; but she said that people couldn't tell what they really were till they were out in the busy world and tried, and that I must be tried before she could venture to marry me. At first I thought her terms very hard; but I do assure you, sir, when I came to know more of the Gospel I felt that they were wise and just. It's a very different thing to appear all right and correct, and to feel very good too, in a quiet village, with a religious, sensible young woman to watch over one, than to keep straight aboard a man-of-war among a number of godless associates. In one case a man may almost forget the necessity of earnest prayer. I do assure you sir, I have felt aboard here that I could not get on an hour without it."

Reader, remember these words of Ellis. Consider how you will act when you are tried and tempted. Satan often lets people alone when he finds them in an easy position, that they may grow conceited of their own strength. Never cease praying that you may see his wiles, and that, through the Holy Spirit, you may be enabled to resist them, but never, never trust to your own strength, or you will be sure to fall.

Some two years after this, when Harry Lethbridge had grown into a fine young man, promising to be as smart an officer as any in the navy, we were on our passage between the northern and southern portions of our station, when we were caught in as heavy a gale as I ever experienced—a complete hurricane. It came down on us so suddenly that it required all hands to shorten sail as smartly as they could do. Among those who sprang aloft when the hands were turned up was Harry Lethbridge, whose station was the foretop. The post of honour among seamen in reefing sails is the weather earing. [Note. An earing is a rope to haul up the outer part of a sail.] Thus when the fore-topsail was to be reefed, Harry eagerly sought, and was the first man out on, the yard-arm. While reefing the sail, on hauling out the earing, from the strength of the wind, and from his anxiety to get it done quickly, he did not haul the first turn sufficiently taut. After taking the second, and getting a good pull on it, the first earing rendered suddenly, and, losing his balance, he fell over the yard. Those who saw him as I did thought he was gone, but no; as he fell he had kept hold of the earing, and there he hung, suspended by it about nine feet below the yard-arm and full sixty from the deck, though, of course, far outside it, that is to say, over the boiling ocean.

Those on deck looked up, almost paralysed with the terrible spectacle. His destruction seemed inevitable. His hands were giving way. He caught the rope in his teeth, and thus he hung suspended, alive and strong, with the joyous spirits and anticipations of youthful manhood, and yet with death as it were gaping for him. The man nearest to him on the yard threw towards him the end of a rope, but it was blown away to leeward out of his reach. The captain instantly directed that a running bowline knot should be made round the earing, and thus lowered over his head; but his voice was drowned by the gale. Cries of horror escaped from the lips of all who saw him. "A man overboard! a man overboard!" was shouted out, for every one expected to see him fall into the sea. William Ellis had never taken his eye off him. I saw him hurry forward. Poor Harry could hold on no longer. His hands relaxed their gripe of the rope, his teeth gave way, he fell. As he did so, the ship lurched heavily to leeward and he came towards the forecastle. Ellis sprang forward, and as Harry's feet touched the deck, caught him in his arms. The midshipman's life was preserved, and the only injury he received was the fracture of one of his ankle-bones. [Note. The whole of this account is fact, without the slightest alteration.] "He's the only man who could have done it, though," I afterwards heard some of the seamen remark. "He prayed that he might do it, and he did it, do ye see." Even the irreligious often acknowledge the efficacy of the prayers of Christian men.

William Ellis persevered in his Christian course till the ship was paid off, when I saw his Mary, who had come to Portsmouth to welcome him. They married; he obtained a warrant as a gunner, and some years afterwards, through the influence of Harry Lethbridge, got a good appointment on shore. The young midshipman, feeling that his life had, through God's mercy, been preserved that he might do Him service, became a thorough Christian, in practice as well as in name, and a first-rate officer; while Ellis continued as he had begun, aided and encouraged, I have no doubt, by his excellent wife, to the end of his life.

* * * * *

Note. This account was given to the author by the late Admiral Saumarez, and the words are to the best of his recollection those used by the man who performed the act recorded.

CHAPTER SEVEN

THE TWO SAILOR-BOYS, A TRUE TALE

NED BURTON LOSES HIS MOTHER, AND IS LEFT PENNILESS—WALKS TO PORTSMOUTH, AND IS DISHEARTENED—IS CHEERED, DIRECTED, AND HELPED BY OLD MOLL—GETS ON BOARD THE TRAINING SHIP—AND MAKES A FRIEND—BUT IS REJECTED FOR NOT BEING ABLE TO READ— COMFORTED BY BILL HUDSON—BILL'S SHIPMATES HELP NED TO FIELD LANE—BILL TAKES HIM THERE—HE IS KINDLY RECEIVED— IS MADE A SAILOR OF AT LAST

On a miserable pallet bedstead, in a small attic of one of the meanest houses in the lowest portion of a provincial town in the south of England, a woman lay dying. The curtainless window and window—panes, stuffed with straw, the scanty patchwork covering to the bed, the single rickety chair, the unswept floor, the damp, mildewed walls, the door falling from its hinges, told of pinching poverty. On the opposite corner to the bedstead there was a heap of straw, to serve as another bed, and against the wall a much-battered sea-chest and an open basket, containing even now a few rotting oranges, some damaged tapes, and such articles as are vended by small hawkers. Standing by the bed-side was a lad with an intelligent, not ill-favoured, countenance, though sickly, and expressive of deep grief, as he gazed on the face of one who had ever been a kind mother to him, and from whom he now knew full well that he was to be parted for ever.

"Ned, my boy, I have done my best to keep myself and thee from the workhouse," said the woman, trying to lift herself up on her arm, that she might the better see the lad. "It has been a hard struggle, but I have done it for thy father's sake. He was a sailor, and would never have thought to see me come to this pass. Thou must be one, too, Ned. It's a rough life, but better far than starving on shore. I've done little for thee, lad, but feed thee, and try to teach thee to be honest, as thy father was. Be honest, Ned, whatever ye do, for thy poor mother's sake. But for thee, lad, I'd have left the weary world many a long year ago."

"Oh, mother, mother, stay now—oh, do!" cried the lad. "Won't the doctor help you—won't the parson?"

"No, lad; no doctor, no parson, can keep me here. But I'd like to see the parson. Maybe he'd tell me about the place I'm going to; for it's far off, I wot, and little I know of the road."

"Oh, mother, I'll run and fetch him."

Just as Ned was going, the dying woman sunk down, exhausted with talking. "Don't leave me, boy," she faintly murmured; "it's too late now. May God hear a widow's prayer, and be merciful to you, and forgive me."

Her voice sank—the last words were gasped out. Her son bent his head to hear her: he stood gazing at her face, expecting to hear her speak again. Gradually he became aware that he was alone in the world. His grief was too deep for tears. For hours he stood there, watching the face of the only being who had cared for him in the world; and then Ned Burton went out and did as she had before bade him, and, with the money she had hoarded up for the purpose, and that produced by the sale of the last few articles in the house, save his father's sea-chest, obtained for her an humble funeral, truly, but not that of a pauper. Then, leaving the chest with a neighbour till he should return and claim it, he went forth penniless into the world to seek his fortune.

Ned Burton's ambition was to be a sailor—not that he knew anything of the sea, except that his father had spent his life on it. His mother could not read or write, and, unable to instruct him or to pay for his instruction, being, indeed, too poor to do without the pittance his labours brought, she had allowed him to grow up in extreme ignorance— though, according to the faint light that was in her, she had taught him, to the best of her power, to do right. Still, poor Ned knew nothing of religion. He had never been taught even to pray. Thus, helpless and forlorn, he went forth to battle with the world. A neighbour had told him that big ships sailed from Portsmouth, so towards Portsmouth he bent his steps, inquiring his way as he went. A few of those who knew him, and had bought his mother's oranges and bobbins, gave him a few pence, and filled his wallet with crusts of bread, and scraps of cheese and bacon, so that he had not to beg for food.

At night he slept under haystacks or hedges, or in empty barns, and thus in time he reached Portsmouth, sore-footed, weary, and hungry, for during the last day his wallet had been empty.

Wandering down the High Street, he passed through a large gateway, and out on a common, from whence he caught sight of the blue sea, and several huge ships floating on it, but they were too far out to reach, and he had no money to pay for a boat; and he would have gained nothing had he reached them, for a poor ragged boy like him would not have been received on board. So he went back the way he had come. He asked several people if they could tell him how he could get on board ship, but they must have thought that he was silly, for they smiled and passed on.

He had begun to think that he should never obtain his wishes, when close to the Southsea Gate he saw an old apple-woman sitting at her stall. She brought his mother to mind. She looked kind, too, so he asked her. Something in his manner touched Old Moll's heart. She asked him several questions, and then said, "Sure, yes; there's what they call a training-ship for boys—the old—, off the Dockyard, at Portsea. They, maybe, will take you. Here's sixpence to get aboard; and here—you look hungry, lad—is some ginger-bread and apples—they'll do you good; and now God speed you! Go straight on—you can't miss the way, and come and tell me some day how you've fared."

Ned went on through narrow lanes and dirty streets, till he came near the shore of the harbour, which was crowded with vessels of all sizes.

"If one won't have me, surely another will," he said to himself, as he gazed with wonder at some of the line-of-battle ships. "They must want a precious number of people to fill those great things."

He now began to inquire which was the old —, where boys were received. He was told that he couldn't see her from there—that she was higher up the harbour; but none of the boatmen he spoke to seemed disposed to take him on board. In vain he promised his sixpence. He had gone out to the end of one of the slips from the Common Hard, when two

W. H. G. Kingston

seamen and a sailor lad came down, carrying baskets, evidently full of provisions, and directed one of the boatmen who had just refused him to take them on board the old —. As they were stepping into the wherry, the boatman beckoned to Ned, and told him that he could now go. He took his seat next to the lad, who, in spite of his own clean white trousers, and blue shirt with worked collar, and fresh straw hat, seemed in no way to despise his ragged dress. In a kind tone he asked Ned why he was going on board. Ned told him.

"Hope you'll succeed, mate," he observed. "A year ago, I was like you—only paler and thinner, and maybe fewer clothes to my back—and trembled when I went aloft; and now there are not many aboard can reach the main-truck from the deck before me, or lay out smarter on a yard."

The tide was against them, so that Ned had time to tell his new acquaintances a good deal of his history before they reached the ship. They all seemed to take an interest in him, especially the lad—a fine, strong ruddy-faced young fellow of sixteen.

"Well, just do you ask for Bill Hudson—that's me—after you've seen the first lieutenant and the doctor; and then I'll tell you what to do," said the latter. "You might lose yourself, do ye see, otherwise, about there."

When they arrived alongside the huge ship, and Ned proffered his sixpence, the men wouldn't let him pay it, but helped him up the side through the entrance port, when he found himself, for the first time, on the main-deck of a man-of-war. While Bill Hudson went to find the proper person to take him to the officers for examination, he was lost in wonder, looking at the huge guns, with their polished gear, the countless number, it seemed, of boys and men moving about—all so cleanly and neatly dressed—and the spotless decks, white as a wooden platter.

At length he was summoned. He trembled with agitation, for he felt so dirty, and poor, and miserable, that he thought the officers, when they saw him, would quickly turn him out of the ship again. The first lieutenant, however, important as he looked, seemed pleased with his appearance and manner; the surgeon pronounced him a healthy, able-bodied lad, fit for the service; but he had brought no certificates of parentage or age. Had he his parents' permission to come to sea? he was asked. They were both dead: he had no friends; but he produced a tin case which had been his father's. The contents showed that the owner had been a petty officer in the navy, and had borne an excellent character. But another question was put; could he read and write? (No boys could be received at that time unless they possessed those accomplishments.) Poor Ned had to confess that he was ignorant of both arts.

He was finally rejected. There was no help for it; though, as his father's certificate-case was returned to him, the officers expressed a hope that he might be some day accepted, if he could learn.

He went forward, much dejected, to find Bill Hudson; for this was but small consolation to him. How could he learn to read and write, when all his strength would be required to obtain food for his subsistence? So he thought.

Bill heard his account of what had happened.

"If you had said that you couldn't read and write, I could have told you what would happen. But, don't be cast down, Ned. Little more than three years ago, I couldn't read nor write, and hadn't shoes to my feet, and scarce a rag on my back. I was a poor outcast boy, without father or mother—no shelter for my head, and often no food to eat. I picked up a living as I could, holding horses, running errands, when anybody would trust me. I didn't steal, but I was often and often very near doing so, as I passed the butchers', and fruiterers', and bakers' shops—just to fill my empty stomach. It wasn't so much because I wouldn't do it, as because I knew that they kept a sharp look-out, and I should have been caught. At last I thought I would try it on; and I didn't care if I was sent to prison, for I should have been fed, at all events: but that very day a gentleman passing, saw me watching a stall, the owner of which had just left it, as if I was going to take whatever I could grab; and so I was. And he asked me if I was hungry; and he gave me a roll from his pocket, and then he asked me where I lived, and I said 'Nowhere;' and then he told me that if I would follow him he would show me where I could get food and shelter, and, might be, clothing and instruction, and means, too, of gaining my livelihood. Though I didn't much credit him, I went; and he took me to the Field Lane Ragged School, as it is called; and there I found all he told me, and more. I soon showed them that I didn't want to eat the bread of idleness, and they got me employment in the day, and in the evening I used to go regularly to the school, and sleep in the Refuge, till I earned enough, by working four days, to go to the day-school for two days; and I soon learned to read and write; and more than that, Ned, I learned what made me a Christian, which I wasn't before I went there. For, I tell you, Ned, I was a heathen; I knew no more about God and his love for man than a block of stone; and I thought that he hated poor people, and sent them all to hell, and that there was no use being good. I did not know that it was sin brought the misery I saw around me into the world, and that God hates sin, but loves sinners; for if he doesn't, he'd never have sent his only Son into the world to save them. At last I was asked what trade I would be, and I said, 'A sailor;' for I had been reading about the sea, and thought I should like to live on it. So they sent me down here, and I do like it, Ned, right well. And now I've told you all this, because I want to ask you if you'd like to go to Field Lane. I tell you it is a blessed place; and a blessed moment it was to me when I entered it. You'd learn to read and write, and be looked after, and learn to gain your daily bread, and be told about God and Jesus Christ, and how to be happy; and if you don't know about them, you can't be happy, that I tell you."

Ned had been much surprised with all he had seen on board ship, but he was more surprised at what Bill told him, though in a different way. He said, certainly that he should like to go there, but how could he? Bill replied that "where there's a will there's a way." Many of his shipmates had heard Ned's history, and were interested in him; and he would speak to the first lieutenant and to some of the officers, who were kind, Christian men, and see what could be done.

Bill Hudson did do his best, and very effectual that was. He had acted as officer's servant, and saved up some money; and he went round the ship and told Ned's story; and all who heard it subscribed—some more and some less; and the officers, when they heard his proposal, subscribed very liberally. Ned was invited down to Bill's mess, and never had he eaten so hearty a dinner.

"No wonder the sailors on board here grow stout and strong, if they have so good a dinner as this every day," he observed.

"It's the same every day. No banyan days with us, now, in the navy," was the answer.

At last Bill Hudson's plan was matured, and the power granted him for carrying it into execution. Ned was told he

W. H. G. Kingston

must stop on board for tea. In the evening Bill came to him triumphant.

"It's all settled," he exclaimed. "You see, Ned, it would never do for you to go up to big London all by yourself, and to wander about, not knowing your way; so I've got leave from the first lieutenant to go with you."

"You—you go up to London with me; that will be good!" exclaimed Ned, delighted.

Ned slept on board, and, from the kind way he was treated, wished more than ever to go to sea. He was not aware—happily for himself—that he could have gone to sea, in the merchant service, without being able to read, and that only at that time, when it was resolved to raise the character of the men in the navy, that the rule with regard to reading and writing was enforced.

The next morning—Ned having been supplied, by the contributions of the sailors, with a suit of clothes, a pair of shoes, and a hat, and some shirts and other things in a bundle—the two lads left the ship, and took the first train to London. Bill would have gladly gone on foot, for the sake of economising his funds, so as to leave more with his new friend; but his leave extended only over three days, and he had many things to do.

The boys arrived in due time at London, and Bill employed as much time as he could in showing Ned about town. As evening drew on they repaired to Field Lane, and knocked for admission at the Refuge.

"What? William Hudson come back! What has happened to you, lad?" exclaimed the porter.

"Yes; it's myself, sure enough. I've come back to ask for a night's lodging, if there's room, and to bring this boy, who wants one badly. Can I see the superintendent?"

"Yes, sure. You know the way, Bill; go on," said the porter, in a kind tone.

The superintendent was very much pleased to see Bill Hudson, and more so to hear the story with which he introduced Ned Burton. He promised, gladly, to look after Ned, and, if he behaved well, to obtain regular employment for him in the neighbourhood.

Bill found, on calculating the amount of his funds, that he might leave some with the superintendent for Ned's use.

"I don't distrust you, Ned; but London is an awful wicked place; and if you kept the money, it might be stolen, and you almost murdered for the sake of it," he observed.

The next day the lads went out together, that Bill might introduce Ned to some of the people who used to employ him. Some had forgotten him; some had gone away; but a few remembered him kindly, and promised to help Ned.

Ned could not help shedding tears when Bill wrung his hand, as he was about to start back for Portsmouth. Then, if it had not been for the Refuge, and the superintendent, and the good missionary, and the porter, he would indeed have felt very miserable and forlorn, in the big city; but Field Lane was now to him his home, indeed—his refuge from adversity.

He remembered, however, that he had to work; so he set about finding employment in good earnest. His decent dress and manner were in his favour; and he gained a few pence,

W. H. G. Kingston

though, being a stranger, not so much as he might have gained had he known the ways of London. At night he went back to the Refuge with a thankful heart, and commenced his schooling. He gave his mind to his task, though he found it very hard work, at first, even learning the letters. The next night it was easier, and he was soon able, when waiting for a job, to employ himself by spelling out the names over the shop doors and the words on the advertising papers. Sometimes he could get nothing to do, especially in very bad weather; and then he went to the industrial school at the Refuge, if it was open, or to the day-school; and here he began to understand the great truths about religion, of which he had before been entirely ignorant. To one of the missionaries, who was especially kind to him, he took a great fancy; and to this good man he used to go, whenever he had an opportunity, and ask him questions, and to listen to his addresses. He first here heard the glorious tidings that "God is love;" and as he saw that beautiful principle carried out in every department of the undertaking, he could not help saying, "Ay, truly, this is God's work."

In little more than a year he had learned, by diligent attention, not only to read well, but to write a fair hand, while he had added greatly to his religious and secular knowledge; and, above all, he had become a new creature in Christ Jesus.

One day he received a letter at the Refuge from Bill Hudson. Bill wrote that he had just arrived at Portsmouth in the frigate to which he now belonged, and that if Ned would come down at once, he would see him on board the old—, where he was sure that he would be received. Bill, moreover, enclosed a sovereign to pay for his journey.

Ned was sorry to leave the Refuge, and yet he rejoiced at the thought of being now able, as he had so long wished, to go to sea. His parting from his friends and journey to Portsmouth need not be described. Bill was at the station to meet him, and at once went with him on board the old —.

He was, without difficulty, accepted. Bill had advised him to show his father's certificates. The first lieutenant spoke to him very kindly, when he saw them, and told him that he had known his father, who was a very good man, and he hoped that Ned would follow his example.

Ned Burton was no longer only a good-natured, well-meaning lad; he had now right principles to help him behave well; nor has he in any way disappointed the hopes of those who have taken an interest in his welfare.

W. H. G. Kingston

CHAPTER EIGHT

THE GOOD CAPTAIN

THE MUTINY AT SPITHEAD—AN EXCEPTION— VALUE OF A CHRISTIAN CAPTAIN—THE MUTINY BREAKS OUT AT SHEERNESS—ANOTHER LOYAL SHIP—THE MUTINY QUELLED

In the year 1797 an event occurred connected with the navy of England, which cannot even now be thought of without sorrow and shame. The crews of most of the ships of the Channel fleet then anchored at Spithead deposed their officers, and refused to proceed to sea, unless certain grievances of which they complained were redressed.

It must be remembered, however, that the seamen of those days were very uneducated—too often utterly ignorant of religious truth, and thus easily imposed upon by designing men. Their pay was scanty, the provisions served out to them often bad, and deficient in quantity, while no care was taken of their moral or spiritual welfare. Still no excuse can be offered for mutiny however much we may pity those who are induced to commit the crime in the hopes of obtaining redress for wrongs. The Christian must ever look to his Lord and Master, and be guided by His conduct under wrong and oppression. However, all the ships' companies did not mutiny, and among those which remained faithful to their duty was the crew of the *Saint Fiorenzo* frigate, Captain Sir Harry Burrard Neale. How came this about? Was discipline less strict on board the *Saint Fiorenzo*? Were her crew allowed greater licence than those of other ships? Certainly not. But on board her the law of kindness, of mercy, and justice prevailed; on board many others it was too often neglected. However, an account of the behaviour of her crew on that trying occasion shall be given in the words of one who was then a midshipman on board her:—

"Our captain was one of the most upright and humane men in the service— a perfect officer and a perfect gentleman;" and a true, humble Christian, from whose mouth an oath never proceeded, whose lips never uttered a falsehood, might have been added. "He was a great favourite with George the Third, and the *Saint Fiorenzo* had consequently been appointed to attend on His Majesty during his summer sojourn at Weymouth. The King won the affection of both officers and men by his urbane and kind manners whenever he came on board. He used to call us up, and talk to us, lieutenants, midshipmen, and seamen alike, in the most familiar manner, taking an interest in our private histories, and all we had to say for ourselves. No wonder, then, that officers and men were loyal to the back-bone. Our captain, too, from the day he commissioned the ship, had, by his justice and kindness, done still more to make the officers and men love him. Few fathers would have been more thoughtful of the interests of their children than he was of the welfare of the men under his charge. On the 14th of April, 1797, the *Saint Fiorenzo* lay at Spithead, forming one of a large fleet under Lord Bridport. It was known that certain complaints had been sent up to the Admiralty by the ships' companies, but little was thought of the matter by the officers, when some of the petty officers of the *Saint Fiorenzo* informed Sir Harry that the men of most of the ships had resolved to

W. H. G. Kingston

mutiny, if the complaints were not forthwith attended to. It was supposed that the documents received at the Admiralty were forgeries, or sent up by a few disaffected men. Sir Harry, however, on cross-questioning our people, was convinced that the petitions really did express the opinions of the seamen of the navy, and promising that he would make the true state of the case known, that very evening sent up an officer with despatches to London. The next day the mutiny broke out, and each ship's company was directed to send representatives, called delegates, on board the *Queen Charlotte*. Sir Harry directed our ship's company to select two of the most sensible and trustworthy of our men, Aynsley and Stanley, as their delegates, and they regularly informed him of all that was taking place. His representations had great weight at head-quarters; the more reasonable demands of the mutineers were granted, and the seamen returned to their duty.

"In the meantime we received orders to fit out at Sheerness, to carry over the Princess Royal to Cuxhaven, after her marriage with the Duke of Wurtemburg. That no time might be lost, the guns on both sides, from the cabin door to the break of the poop, were sent down into the hold, that the carpenters might begin fitting up the cabins, thus crippling our powers as a fighting ship.

"On our arrival at Sheerness, great was our astonishment at finding the red flag—the signal of mutiny—flying on board the *Sandwich*. It being supposed that her crew had not been informed of what had taken place at Spithead, our delegates were sent to explain matters. On getting on board they were disgusted to find that fresh demands had been made on the Government by the crews of the North Sea fleet, of a nature so frivolous that they were not at all likely to be granted. Our men, it appeared, expressed their views in a very unguarded way, and in no courteous language. This enraged Parker—

the unhappy man who had assumed the command of the fleet—and the other ringleaders, and our ship's company became marked as disaffected to the common cause. From the information our delegates gave on their return, it was suspected that the mutineers intended removing our officers. In consequence, Sir Harry resolved immediately to quit the fleet and to run into the harbour of Sheerness.

"Near us lay the *Clyde*, an old fellow-cruiser, commanded by Captain Cunningham, who had, also, by kindness and justice, won the confidence and affection of his crew. An arrangement was accordingly made between the two captains and the ship's companies, that they would make the attempt together, and share each other's fortune.

"Neither of our pilots, however, through fear or treachery, would take charge of the ships. At this juncture Captain Cunningham went on board the *Chatham* yacht, which lay near, for Mr William Bardo, one of her mates with whose fitness for the task he was acquainted. Mr Bardo undertook the task of piloting the *Clyde*, and as she was the inshore ship, she was to move first. We watched her with intense anxiety. She cast the right way, and before one of the ships in the power of the mutineers could make sail after her, she was safe from pursuit. Not having a pilot we could trust, and the tide now being unfavourable, Sir Harry decided to wait till the suspicions of the mutineers might be lulled. Our anxiety was relieved when, soon after dusk, Mr Bardo, sent by Captain Cunningham, came off to us in a small boat to pilot us in. Just, however, as we were preparing to move the next morning, a body of the delegates came on board, and, abusing our men for allowing the *Clyde* to escape without firing into her, ordered them to bring the *Saint Fiorenzo* in and place her between the *Inflexible* and *Director*, to unbend our sails, and to send our gunpowder on board the *Sandwich*, the flag-ship of the so-called Admiral Parker. So enraged were our people with these orders, that one of the quarter-masters, John Aynsley, came aft, and in the name of the ship's company, begged that they might heave the delegates overboard.

"Sir Harry, however, to whom all matters were referred, while he sat quietly in his cabin out of sight, ordered our delegates to express their readiness to comply with Admiral Parker's orders; and at length the mutineers, satisfied that we were about to do as directed, left the ship.

"As soon as they were gone, we got springs on our cable, so as to cast inwards, and all was made ready to run, as was at first intended, into Sheerness. In heaving, however, the spring broke, and we cast outward. The effect of this was to carry us right among the mutinous fleet.

"At this critical juncture, Sir Harry, whose presence of mind never forsook him, directed one of the quartermasters to appear on deck as if in command, while he and all the officers concealed themselves in different parts of the ship—he posting himself so that he could, unseen, issue his orders. In a moment every sail was sheeted home, and we stood in between the two line-of-battle ships, which, as the delegates had told us, had all their guns double shotted, while their crews stood ready, lanyards in hand, to sink us with their broadsides.

"On we stood, the ship gathering good way, when, as we got in among the mutinous fleet, Sir Harry gave the order to let fly all the sheets. This so completely took the mutineers by surprise that they, believing the ship was coming about, did not fire a shot at us. Sir Harry then ordered the helm to be put 'hard a port,' which caused the ship to shoot ahead of the *Inflexible* and clear of her. He immediately sprang on deck, crying out, 'Well done, my lads!' A loud murmur of applause was heard fore and aft along the deck, but we had no time for cheering. 'Now clear away the bulk-heads, and mount the guns,' he added. Scarcely were the words out of his mouth, than the whole fleet of thirty-two sail opened their fire. The shot fell thick as hail around us on every side. The men stood at their stations without flinching. Of course it would have been worse than useless to have returned their fire.

"On we stood. Never ship passed through such a fire so slightly scathed. Not that we escaped altogether; now a shot struck us, now another. The *Director* alone might have sunk us; but, as far as we could judge, not a shot came from her. Some believed that her crew, struck with admiration at the heroism displayed by our people, fired wide, or did not put shot into their guns. Though we were repeatedly hulled, not a rope was shot away, nor was any one hurt on board. God in his mercy, working as he thinks fit to work through human agency, protected us. Everybody was labouring with a will, and in two hours we had our decks clear, our guns mounted, and were in a perfect state of preparation to meet a foe.

"No sooner was this done than the men came aft in a body, and begged Sir Harry that should any of the mutinous fleet come up with us, they might be allowed to go down at their guns rather than return to the Nore. The captain promised them that they should have their wish: at which they seemed as contented as if some great favour had been done them.

"As yet, however, there were no signs of our being pursued: though shortly the determination of our men was to be put to the test.

"Sir Harry had resolved to return to Portsmouth, and when just off the mouth of the Thames a fleet of men-of-war hove in sight. They approached with the red flag at their mast-heads. This was the North Sea fleet, with the admiral and all

W. H. G. Kingston

the officers under arrest.

"No sooner were we seen than a frigate bore down on us. That we could escape her was doubtful; and though we could have beaten her off had we fired, we should have brought the rest of the fleet down on us. Sir Harry, therefore, gave the speaking-trumpet to Stanley, and directed him to answer the questions of the mutineers. His replies seemed satisfactory, for the frigate, hauling her wind, rejoined the fleet. Scarcely had we lost sight of the North Sea fleet, than we spoke a brig, which gave us the astounding information that the mutiny had again broken out at Spithead. We therefore, just as it was growing dark, anchored under Dungeness, with springs on our cables, prepared for an attack.

"Towards the end of the middle watch, a large ship, as she appeared, was seen bearing down towards us. The crew, believing her to be a foe, again came aft, and repeated their request to be allowed to sink, rather than surrender to the mutineers. The private signals were made: they were answered; but that was no security, as the mutineers would of course have possessed themselves of them. The drum beat to quarters. It was a time of awful suspense. The wind was very light. The stranger closed slowly. Many asserted that she was a line-of-battle ship. As the light from our fighting-lanterns beamed forth from every port, it was easily seen what we were. Our springs were hove on, to keep our broadside to bear. Our captain hailed; breathless, we waited for a reply. The answer was, 'H.M.S. *Huzzar*, Captain Lord Garlais, from the West Indies.' Coming from a long voyage, she was high out of the water, which made her appear, in the gloom, like a line-of-battle ship. When his people, who had heard nothing of the mutiny, were acquainted with what had occurred, they were so much struck with the bravery and determination of our ship's company, that they promised to stick by us, and share our fate if attacked by the mutineers.

Not many days after this, Parker and his associates were allowed by the seamen they had misled to be carried on shore by a file of soldiers, without opposition, and the mutiny was brought to an end."

The last years of that good captain, who had been the friend and companion of princes—who had so often in battle met the enemies of his country, were spent in visiting the cottages of the poor surrounding his house, telling them of the Saviour's love, carrying them food and clothing, and other comforts, and never failing to speak kind words of comfort and advice.

But we must not pause here. Some important lessons are to be learnt from this narrative. See how the law of love and kindness, combined with justice, prevails, where harshness and severity fail. The crews of the *Saint Fiorenzo* and *Clyde* were composed of the same class of men as those of the ships which mutinied; yet the latter basely struck their colours, and the former were ready to die for their officers.

Let us ask ourselves, how do we rule in our families—over those placed under us? By the rule of our merciful Saviour, or by the rule of the world, of our own tempers—that is, the flesh—or of the devil?

See, again, by the way the crew of the *Huzzar* behaved, what a good example can effect. If we adhere to the Captain of our Salvation—firmly and boldly confess him—we may be assured that we not only shall gain the respect of our associates, but, which is of far more consequence, that we shall bring over others to love and confess him also.

Then, again, can we, after reading this account, think without sorrow and confusion of the way we have behaved to our heavenly King and Captain? We are told that because the

W. H. G. Kingston

king spoke to the officers and crew of the *Saint Fiorenzo* in a kind manner, taking an interest in their private histories, they were loyal to the backbone. Does not our heavenly King and Father speak to us daily, through the Holy Scriptures, words full of kindness, love, and mercy? Surely he does, if we will but diligently read that Book of books. He allows us, too, as no earthly king can do, to go to him daily—every hour—every moment of our lives. His ear is ever open to our prayers—he who keeps Israel neither slumbers nor sleeps—to tell him our private histories—our wants, our wishes, our hopes; to confess to him all we have done amiss—all our sins. And, moreover, he promises us that if we repent of them, and trust to the cleansing blood of Jesus, he will forgive them freely and fully, and give us what no earthly monarch can give, eternal life, and raise us to dwell with him in happiness unspeakable, for ever and ever.

CHAPTER NINE

THE SMUGGLER'S FATE

THE SMUGGLER'S WIFE—HANSON STARTS ON HIS TRIP—HIS WIFE'S ANXIETY—THE REVENUE OFFICERS APPROACH—THE SMUGGLERS TAKE TO THE WATER—THE FIGHT—A FEARFUL END

"Good-bye, Susan—good-bye, my wife. I'll bring thee over a silk gown, and such Brussels lace as you've never yet set eyes on. It will make a lady of you; and you're not far off being one now, to my mind, so don't fret—don't fret, Susan, dear."

These words were uttered by Robert Hanson, a fine sailor-like-looking man. And a bold seaman he was, indeed; but was also unhappily known to be one of the most daring smugglers on the coast. Having kissed his wife affection-ately, and knelt down by the side of the cradle in which their infant slept, to bestow another kiss on its smiling lips, he hurried from the cottage.

Susan looked after him sorrowfully. She had entreated him, over and over again—not as earnestly as she might, perhaps —to give up his dangerous and lawless occupation, and with a laugh he had told her that each trip should be his last. Did it

W. H. G. Kingston

never occur to him how his promise might be fulfilled? It did to Susan; and often and often she had trembled at the thought. She had been brought up by praying parents, and had been taught from her childhood to pray, but she could not pray now—she dared not—she felt it would be a mockery. She was wrong, though. She could not pray that God would protect her husband in his lawless occupation, but she might have prayed that her merciful Father in heaven would change his heart—would lead him from the paths of sin, and put a right spirit within him, even although he might be brought to poverty, and she might no longer enjoy the luxuries which he allowed her. She was sure, however, that he could make, by a lawful calling, enough for all their wants; whereas a large portion of what he now gained was spent in feasting and treating with open hand his smuggling companions; so at the end of the year, except for the dresses and other articles which were utterly useless to Susan, they were very little the better for all his toil and the many fearful risks he had run. She stood watching him with tearful eyes and a foreboding heart, as he descended the cliff on which their cottage stood.

Bob, as Hanson was called by his companions, looked in at three or four of the huts which formed the fishing village at the foot of the cliff, and gave sundry directions to their inmates. The answer he received from all of them was much the same: "Never fear, captain, we'll be ready."

"You understand, Dore," he said, stopping at one of the huts for some little time, "you'll be on the look-out for us on Tuesday night at Durlstone Point. Now mind you also tell Green, the landlord of the 'Jolly Tar,' to have the two covered carts there, with his fastest horses and trusty men to drive—Bill Snow and Tom Thatcher—they are true men; but not that fellow Dennis—he'll bring the Coast Guard down on us one of these days, you'll see, if we trust him—and take care that we've no lack of hands to run the cargo up the cliff."

Such were some of the directions Hanson gave to his confederates. He then, with active steps, proceeded to a small harbour at a little distance along the shore, where a fast-looking cutter of about forty tons lay at anchor. He hailed her. A preventive man (as the revenue officers are called), with his spyglass under his arm, passed him.

"What, Bob, off again?" he said, in a careless tone; "we'll be on the look-out for you, if you'll tell us when you are coming back."

"May be next week, or the week after, or a month from this; but thank you all the same," answered Bob, laughing, as he stepped into the punt which came for him. As soon as he was on board, the *Saucy Sue* made sail for the French shore, and, under a crowd of canvas, was soon out of sight.

It was soon known at each preventive station along the coast that Bob Hanson was away in the *Saucy Sue*, and might ere long be expected back with a cargo of contraband. A sharp look-out was accordingly kept for him. Often and often before this, however, he had been expected, but the goods had been run, notwithstanding, and the *Saucy Sue* having appeared in the offing, had come into the harbour without an article of contraband on board, Bob and his crew looking innocent as lambs.

Tuesday came. Susan knew that on that night the attempt to run the cargo was to be made. There was no moon. The sun set red and lowering over Durlstone Point, and dark clouds were seen chasing each other rapidly across the sky, rising from a dark bank which rested on the western horizon, while white-crested seas began to rise up out of the sombre green ocean, every instant increasing in number. The wind whistled mournfully among the bushes and the few stunted trees, with tops bending inland, which fringed the cliffs, and the murmur of the waves on the beach below changed ere long into a ceaseless roar.

Susan sat in her cottage, watching the last rays of the setting sun as her foot rocked her baby's cradle. She knew well the path to Durlstone Point along the cliffs. No longer able to restrain her anxiety (why more excited than usual on that evening, she could not have told), she left her child in charge of her young sister, who had come in to see her, and hurried out. The clouds came up thicker and thicker from the south-west, and the darkness rapidly increased. She had good reason to dread falling over the cliff. Several times she contemplated turning back; but the thought of her husband's danger urged her on. "If I could find the spotsman, Ned Dore, I would beseech him to warn the cutter off," she said to herself; "it can never be done on a night like this." She went on till she came to a dip, or gulley, when a break in the cliff occurred. A steep path led down the centre to the beach. She heard the sound of wheels, with the stamp of horses' feet, as if the animals had started forward impatiently and been checked, and there was also the murmur of several voices. Suddenly a light flashed close to her.

"Oh, Ned Dore, is that you?" she exclaimed. "Don't let them land to-night; there'll be harm come of it."

"No fear, Mrs Hanson," said Dore, recognising her voice. "All's right—the cutter has made her signal, and I have answered it. Couldn't have a better time. The revenue men are all on the wrong scent, and we'll have every cask a dozen miles from this before they are back. Just you go home, good woman, and your husband will be there before long."

Susan, however, had no intention of leaving the spot. Again

she entreated Dore, almost with tears, to warn off the cutter, alleging that there was already too much surf on the beach to allow the boats to land with safety. Dore almost angrily again refused, declaring that the cutter had already begun to unload, and that the boats would soon be in. Seeing that her entreaties were useless, she sat herself down on a rock jutting out of the cliff, and tried to peer into the darkness. She waited for some time, when footsteps were heard, and one of the men posted to watch, came running in with the information that a party of the revenue were approaching. Dore, coming up to her, pulled her by force below the rock on which she had been sitting. The other men concealed themselves under the bushes—among other rocks and in holes in the cliff—the lights were extinguished, and the carts were heard moving rapidly away. Not a word was spoken—the men held in their breath as the revenue officers approached. Poor Susan almost fainted with dread—not for herself, but for her husband. Where was he all the time? She knew too well the smugglers' mode of proceeding not to have good cause for fear.

"It was off here, sir, I saw the light flash," Susan heard one of the men say. "There is a road a little further up, and the cart wheels we heard must have passed along it."

"It is a likely spot, and must be watched."

Susan recognised the voice of the last speaker as that of Mr Belland, the new lieutenant of the Coast Guard, reputed to be an active officer.

"Do you, Simpson and Jones, station yourselves on the top of the cliff, and fire your pistols if you see anything suspicious," he said. "Wait an hour, and then move back to your beats—there will be sea enough on by that time to save us further trouble."

W. H. G. Kingston

"Ay, ay, sir," was the brief answer.

The two preventive men took up their stations, one of them directly above where Susan was crouching down, and the lieutenant and his party moved on.

While these events were taking place on shore, the *Saucy Sue* had approached the coast. Her usual signal was made and answered in a satisfactory manner, and preparations for landing the cargo were forthwith commenced. There were among it silks and other valuable articles, carefully packed in water-tight casks. The rest consisted of spirits in casks, two of which a man could carry on his shoulders. The casks were now secured together by ropes in separate parcels, eighteen or two dozen in each, and lowered overboard. The cutter's two boats then took them in tow, and approached the beach. As they drew near, a small light, shown for an instant, warned them that the preventive men were on the alert. A weight sufficient to moor each parcel was on this dropped overboard, and the boats hung on to them.

"We must try the old dodge," said Hanson, after waiting for some time. "I'll take three parcels—Tom and Bill, you take the rest; we've never missed that way."

Saying this, he threw off his outer clothing, the two men he spoke to did the same, and all three slipping overboard, took hold of the tow-lines attached to the casks. The boats returned to the cutter, and were hoisted on board; after which, letting draw her fore-sheet, she stood out at sea. Hanson and his daring companions, buoyed up with a few corks under their arms, and knives in their hands to cut the casks from the moorings, remained with their heads just above the water, watching for the signal to tow them in. There they remained, their eager eyes turned towards the cliff—the dark sky above them, the foaming waters around.

Every instant their position became more perilous; for as the tide rose, the ledge of rocks to the westward no longer afforded them the protection it had done at first, and the seas came rolling in, and the surf broke more and more heavily every instant.

Could they pray for help? No. They knew well that they were engaged in unlawful work—that they were breaking the laws of their country—refusing to render to Caesar the things that were Caesar's. Such was the picture the poor wife beheld in her mind's eye, as she gazed down into the dark waters, where she well knew that her husband then was.

Slowly the anxious hour passed away. The preventive men, however, still seemed suspicious that all was not right, and lingered at their posts. They at last hailed each other, and held a conversation in a low tone. They were close to where two of the men lay hid. Susan, in addition to her other cause of alarm, dreaded that an act of violence would be committed, if they did not move off. The preventive men would fire their pistols, certainly; but there still might be time for the tubs to be landed, and the smugglers to make their escape, before the rest of the Coast Guard could reach the spot. Her alarm increased when she found that Dore had crept away.

What she dreaded happened. The two preventive men came down into the hollow, as if about to descend to the beach. Suddenly they were set upon by a dozen men. One fired his pistol, the other was knocked down before he could draw a weapon from his belt. The first fought desperately, but a blow from a hanger brought him to the ground, where he lay mortally wounded. The arms of the other were pinioned, his mouth gagged, and the smugglers rushed down to the beach.

The signal was now made to Hanson and his companions.

W. H. G. Kingston

The smugglers waited to allow time for them to come in, every instant dreading the return of the Coast Guard. At length a cry was heard, "Help, help!" Several of the most daring rushed into the water. First one of Hanson's companions was dragged on shore, almost exhausted. The tubs were drawn in, and rapidly carried up the cliff. The second man was next found; but he had abandoned his tubs, and was more dead than alive. But where was Hanson himself?

Susan had found her way down to the beach. No one noticed her.

"I'm afraid the captain is gone. It was his plan, but a desperately dangerous one," she heard one of the men say. She stood speechless with terror.

Just then a light flashed from the cliff above.

"Each man for himself," was the cry, as the smugglers made their escape up the only path open to them.

She stood alone on the sand, with the seas roaring up to her feet. She heard footsteps approaching. "Oh! where—where is my husband?" she cried out.

"I don't know, missus; but murder has been committed, and some one has done it." It was one of the preventive men spoke.

Daylight at length broke. A tangled mass of tubs and rope, and a human form attached to them, was seen surging up and down in the foaming breakers. It was dragged on shore, and the poor young widow sank senseless on her husband's body.

CHAPTER TEN

THE INDIAN MOTHER, A TALE OF THE ROCKY MOUNTAINS

THE HALF-BREED TRAPPER LA TOUCHE—HIS WIFE KAMELA—THEIR CHILDREN—THEY ARE SENT ON AN EXPEDITION—THE ENCAMPMENT— ATTACKED BY BLACKFEET, AND THE MEN SLAIN—THE YOUNG WIDOW FLIES—ALMOST CAPTURED—BACK TO THE FORT—THE REFUGE DESTROYED!—WOLVES—FURTHER FLIGHT— REFUGE AT LAST

Great Britain possesses the sovereignty over a rich extent of country, extending from the Atlantic on the east to the Pacific on the west. Beyond the further shore of Lake Superior is found a region of lakes and rapid rivers, rocks, hills, and dense wood, extending for about 400 miles, nearly up to the Red River or Selkirk settlement. To the west of this, a rich prairie stretches far away up to the foot of the Rocky Mountains, from which the Saskatchewan descends, and, soon becoming a broad river, flows rapidly on to Lake Winnepeg. Other streams descending, find their way into the Polar Sea, or Hudson's Bay. On the west, the Columbia, the Fraser, and others flow, with very eccentric courses, into the Pacific. Besides this, there are numerous lakes divided from

W. H. G. Kingston

each other, in many instances, by lofty mountains and thick forests.

Over the whole of this extensive region the Hudson's Bay Company held, for many years, undivided sway, and kept in its employment large numbers of men—voyageurs, or canoe-men, and hunters—both whites of European descent (chiefly French Canadians), and also half-breeds and Red Indians. The country was inhabited by several nations of Indians, some known as Wood Indians, others as Prairie Indians and these again were divided into tribes or clans, frequently at war with each other; and these wars were cruel in the extreme, often exterminatory, neither age nor sex being spared. Their dress was skins, embroidered with beads, feathers, and porcupine quills. They painted their faces and ornamented their hair in a fantastic manner. Their weapons were the bow and arrow, spears, and hatchets. Their canoes were of birch-bark; their habitations, huts, or wigwams, either of a conical shape, or like a basin reversed, and formed of buffalo-skins and birch-bark. The Indians of the prairie possessed horses, and hunted the buffalo. Those of the woods, having few horses, lived chiefly on deer and smaller game, and cultivated potatoes and Indian corn. They believed in one Great and Good Spirit, and in the existence of numerous evil spirits, whom they feared and endeavoured to propitiate. Missionaries, however, went among them, and many have been brought out of darkness to a knowledge of the truth.

Among the most interesting of the tribes in British North America and the west of the Rocky Mountains are the Cootonais. They are handsome, above the middle size, and, compared with other tribes, remarkably fair; in conversation candid, in trade honest, brave in battle, and devotedly attached to each other and to their country. Polygamy is unknown among them. The greatest neatness and cleanliness are observable about their persons and lodges.

It was among this tribe that Pierre La Touche, a brave young half-breed trapper, sought for a wife. He had not long to wait before he found a maiden whose charms captivated his heart; besides which, she was an accomplished manufacturer of mocassins, snow-shoes, and garments of every description; she could also ride a horse and paddle or steer a canoe; she was fearless in danger, and she had, indeed, been greatly tried; once especially, when a party of Blackfeet, the hereditary enemies of her tribe, had made their way over the mountains to recover some horses which her people had captured. The Cootonais claimed the right of hunting the buffalo to the east of the Rocky Mountains, on the prairies which the Blackfeet considered belonged exclusively to themselves. This was naturally a fertile source of dispute.

Kamela, or the "Young Fawn," the name given to the damsel selected by La Touche, had been well trained to endure all the hardships and privations to which a hunter's wife is invariably exposed.

The usual ceremonies having been gone through, the young Kamela went to La Touche's tent, and became his most loving and devoted wife. He treated her, not as the Indians would—as a slave, but as an equal and a friend, except in the presence of her countrymen, when he assumed the stern, indifferent manner with which they treat their wives. La Touche did not long remain idle; but away over the mountains, and down streams and rapids, across lakes, and through dense forests, he had to travel to join a band of the fur-trading company to which he belonged. Here four or five years of his life were spent; and the once-graceful Kamela had become a mother, with two fine children—Moolak, a boy, and a little Kamela.

W. H. G. Kingston

One day, towards the end of the year, La Touche received orders to join Mr McDonald, a factor, with several other men, to assist in establishing a fort on one of the streams which run into the Fraser River. The spot selected was on a high bluff, with the river flowing at its base. The fort was of a simple construction. It was surrounded by a palisade of stout timbers, fixed deeply in the ground, and united by cross-bars, further strengthened by buttresses, and loop-holed for musketry, with a few light guns to sweep the fort should the enemy break in. The interior consisted of log-huts and storehouses. Such is the style of most of the fur-trading forts. To these forts the Indian hunters bring their furs at periodical seasons, and receive fire-arms and ammunition, tobacco, blankets, hatchets, knives, and other articles in return; and too often, also, the deadly "fire-water."

The fort being finished, the hunters were sent off in parties in different directions to search for game—either for food, or for the furs of the animals. Mr McDonald, sending for La Touche, told him that he must proceed to a spot at the distance of about five days' journey, with provisions for six weeks, accompanied by two other men. "We will take care of your wife and children till you return," he added.

"No, thank you, sir; I prefer having my wife's society. We have gone through many hardships and dangers together; and she will be happier with me, and safer than in the fort," answered the hunter.

"How so, La Touche?" asked the factor.

"Why, sir, I mean that we have enemies—that it is possible the fort may be attacked; and that, if you are not very vigilant, it may be captured by treachery, if not by force," answered La Touche.

"You are plain spoken; but you need not be alarmed about our safety. I have not lived among these Red Skins for eight years or more, without knowing their habits and tricks," answered Mr McDonald. "However, by all means, take your wife and children with you: you can have horses to convey them."

La Touche, thanking the good-natured factor, set off with his companions and wife and children. His wife, from habit, marked well the way they took; indeed, from constantly accompanying her husband, she knew the country as well as he did. They met on their way natives of two or three of the neighbouring tribes; but, as they were well mounted and armed, no one molested them. They had rivers to ford, and hills to climb, and there were woods through which, occasionally, to save a long round, they had to hew their way.

At length the party reached the hunting-ground to which the factor had directed them. Wigwams were erected—conical shaped, and covered with birch-bark—in a nook of the dense grove of cedars, where they would be sheltered from the icy winds of the north; one for La Touche and his family, the other for their companions. While the men went out hunting, Kamela remained at home to cook their provisions, and to look after her children; she also set cunningly-devised traps in the neighbourhood of the wigwams, over which she could watch. She never failed to have a good supper prepared for the hunters on their return home in the evening. She was one evening employed as usual, now lulling her little girl to sleep as the infant lay in its hammock in the wigwam, now attending to the simmering caldron, her quick ear ever on the watch for the footstep of her husband. Suddenly she started. "That is not Pierre's footstep," she muttered; "it is that of a stranger—no; it is Michel's. Alas! he is wounded."

Her fears were not unfounded. In another minute, Michel,

one of the hunters, staggered into her hut, fearfully wounded. No sooner had he entered, than he sank on the ground gasping for breath.

"Fly!" he said; "they are both dead—your husband and Thomas. The Blackfleet have done it. Take the horses—ride direct to McDonald's fort—tell him—Oh! this pain! water, good Kamela!"

Before, however, the water reached his lips, the faithful hunter, who had thus exerted his last remaining strength to save, if possible, the life of his friend's wife and children, fell back, and died.

Kamela lost not a moment in giving way to unavailing grief. Michel's condition too fearfully corroborated his account to allow her to doubt it. Hurrying out, she caught with much difficulty two of the horses; putting a pack on one and a saddle on the other, she loaded the first with her blankets and two buffalo-robes, with some dried salmon and beaver-flesh and flour, and on the other she mounted with her boy before her and little Kamela at her back, and set off at a rapid rate in the direction of McDonald's fort.

She rode as she had never before ridden, scarcely daring to look behind lest she should see some of her dreaded enemies in pursuit. Not for herself did she fear—he that had bound her to earth was gone—but she feared for her beloved little ones, who might fall into the hands of her remorseless foes. Night was rapidly drawing on. The ground was covered with snow. It was bitterly cold; but she was afraid to light a fire, lest it might betray her to those who she was persuaded would be on the search for her. With her axe she quickly cut some boughs and stripped off sufficient bark to form a shelter, and wrapping herself and her children in the blankets she had brought, and tethering the horses close to her, she lay down to wait till morning light should enable her to pursue her journey. Sleep did not visit her eyelids, but anxiously she listened the livelong night for any sounds which might indicate the approach of foes. A wandering pack of wolves might have discovered her; and as she had only a long knife, which she had brought away to defend herself, her prospect of escape was small indeed.

Daylight came at last, and at the first grey streak of light in the eastern sky she was again mounted as before, and on her way towards the fort. She did not draw rein except when necessary to stop and feed the horses. If enemies were following her, she began to hope that she had distanced them. Choosing for her camp at night a sheltered spot in a deep hollow, she ventured to light a small fire, at which she could warm her own and her little one's benumbed limbs and dress some food. She slept, too; but still so heavy was her heart, that she would have welcomed death but for the little ones at her side.

Kamela, too, had a hope beyond the grave. Confused as her notions probably were, she had learned from her husband that the Great Spirit, who made the world, is a God of love, and holiness and purity; that it is not His will that any should perish; that it was man's disobedience brought sin, and suffering, and death into the world, and that God's Own Son came into the world that He might triumph over both. Kamela could, therefore, pray intelligently to that Great Spirit through His Son, who died for the sins of the whole world, for protection and support. Not often has a person been placed in greater peril than was that young Indian woman.

On the evening of the third day, just as she had reached the brow of a hill, she saw galloping towards her a band of warriors. She knew at a glance that they were foes. She trusted that she had not been seen. Rapidly turning her horses round, she galloped down the hill into the thickest part of the wood. Again she watched. The Indians, instead of ascending the hill, as she feared they might do, kept along the valley, and thus did not discover her trail. She emerged from her concealment, and, as long as light lasted, pushed on towards the fort. Once there, she trusted that food and shelter would be found for her little ones. More than once little Moolak asked for his father. Only then did tears start to her eyes. She replied, "He has gone to be with the Great Spirit. We shall go to him some day."

The neighbourhood of the fort was reached; her loved ones would be in safety. She drew in her rein. Anxiously she looked towards the bluff on which the fort had been built. "Surely, it rose above yonder clump of bushes," she said to herself.

She approached cautiously. With a sinking heart she gazed at the spot where the fort had stood. It was there no longer, and, in its place, heaps of charred timber and ashes, the smoke from which still ascended to the sky. There could be no doubt that the fort had been destroyed; perhaps even the enemy were yet in the neighbourhood. Still, some of her friends might have escaped. She turned silently away, resolving to visit the spot as soon as the shades of night should veil her approach. At some little distance was a thick cluster of trees. Retreating to it, she carefully concealed the children and the horses. Then, lying down with her little ones, she waited, with her ear close to the ground, for the return of night.

The hours passed slowly. Not a sound broke the stillness of the evening, save that made by the horses as they stirred up the snow to get at the fresh grass and hay and leaves beneath. She fed her children—they were too well trained to cry out—and, kissing them, and offering up a silent prayer that they may be protected, she set out on her perilous expedition. Her only weapon, besides her axe, was a long knife. Gathering her garments tightly round, as she neared the spot where the fort had stood, she crept silently up. The palisades and log huts were still smouldering, but no human voice could she hear. Cautiously at first, and then louder and louder, she called out the names of Mr McDonald and those she had left with him in the fort. Breathlessly she listened— no one answered to the summons. Again and again she called. A strange cry reached her ears: she knew it well. A sudden breeze at that moment fanned up the embers, and by the bright flames which burst forth she beheld, in the farther-off corner of the fort, a band of prairie wolves wrangling and fighting over a banquet, the nature of which she guessed too well. To that part it was evident her friends had retired, with their faces to the foe, and fought till brought down by over-whelming numbers. At that sad moment a new fear seized her—the cry of the prairie wolf reached her from another point: it came from the wood where she had left her children. She panted with agitation, with dread. Maternal love gave wings to her feet: she flew rather than ran back. She sprang over the fallen logs: she dashed aside the boughs in her way, regardless of the wounds they inflicted. She caught sight of two large wolves stealing towards her children. Were they the first, or had others got there before them? She shrieked out—she shouted—she dashed forward with her weapon to meet the savage brutes. In another moment they would have reached her sleeping infants; but, not waiting her approach, they fled, howling, to join the rest of the pack at the fort. Her children were safe: she clasped them to her bosom. They were all, now, that remained to her on earth. For their sake she resolved to struggle on. But she had a fearful prospect before her. Hundreds of miles from any civilised beings, or from any tribe of natives on whose friendship she could rely; without means of procuring food, starvation stared her in the

W. H. G. Kingston

face. Yet she did not despair. She had the two horses: they must die. She might, perhaps, trap some animals; she must also build a habitation to shelter herself and her little ones. There was work enough before her.

She revolved these matters in her mind during the night. By early dawn she mounted her horse, and, leading the other, rode away from the fatal spot. For two days she travelled on, till she reached a range of hills, among which she believed that she should be safe from discovery. She knew too well that, should she encounter any of her husband's foes, neither her sad history nor her sex could save her from the most cruel treatment—scarcely, indeed, from death. At last she reached the locality she sought, and fixed her abode in a deep hollow in the side of the hill facing the sunny south. She had brought with her some buffalo-robes and deer-skins: with these and a few cedar-branches, and some pine and other bark, she constructed a wigwam by the side of a sparkling stream which burst forth from the mountain-side.

No game was to be found, and she was compelled to kill the horses, and smoke-dry their flesh. Their skins added some-what to the comfort of her hut. For three weary months the poor widow, with her orphans, dragged on a sad existence. She saw her stock of food decreasing, and she might have to travel far on foot before she could reach a place where more could be obtained. May had arrived, and there was no time to be lost; so, packing the remainder of her horse-flesh, with as many of her blankets, and buffalo-robes, and other articles as she could carry, with her youngest child on her back, while she led the other, she commenced her weary march across that wild region of mountains, forests, and streams now known as British Columbia. To no human being had she spoken since her husband's dying comrade warned her to fly.

For days she toiled on over the rough ground, often having to carry the little Moolak, in addition to his sister. She had barely food sufficient for another day, when several grey wreaths of smoke ascending from a valley told her that a band of friends or foes were encamped below. She hesitated to approach them. "They may be foes; and if they are, will they spare me, wretched though I am?" she said to herself. She looked at her children. "I have no more food for them; I must venture on."

Emerging from a thick wood, she saw close before her a large encampment. She staggered forward, and stood trembling amid the camp. A chief stepped forward from his wigwam and listened to her tale, which was soon told.

"You shall be a sister to us," he answered. "Your people are our friends, and, still more, are your husband's people. I will be as a father to your children. Fear not, sister. Here you shall find rest, and shelter, and food."

The chief kept to his word, and the poor widow was treated with the greatest kindness by him and his people. The summer came, and a brigade of the company's trading canoes passed down the river. The people landed, and spoke to her. She was known to several of them, and they invited her to accompany them. The Indians entreated her to remain with them. She thanked them and said, "No, I will go with my husband's people. When I wedded him I became one of them. I wish, also, that his children should become like them, and be brought up in the faith to which he held."

Wishing, therefore, the kind Indians farewell, she accompanied the voyageurs; and in the far-off settlement to the east, where she ultimately took up her abode under a Christian missionary, she herself learned more clearly to comprehend the truths of the Gospel whose gracious offers she had embraced, while by all around she was respected and beloved.

W. H. G. Kingston

CHAPTER ELEVEN

THE TRAWLERS, A TALE OF THE NORTH SEA

THE NORTH SEA FLEET—SUNDAY AT THE FISHING GROUND—THE MISSIONARY SERVICE— THE GALE—A MISHAP TO THE SEA-GULL AND HER CAPTAIN—A CRASH— THE CAPTAIN'S DEATH—ALL LOST BUT TWO BOYS—DOING ONE'S DUTY—MORNING— ALONE WITH A DEAD MAN—BREAKFAST—TO THE PUMPS—SAVED AT LAST

A fleet of a hundred vessels or more lay together, dotting the surface of the German Ocean, or North Sea, as it is more generally called, upwards of 300 miles from the English shore. They were mostly luggers, of from sixty to eighty tons; each with a crew of from seven to nine men. These vessels formed a part of the North Sea fishing fleet, chiefly belonging to Great Yarmouth and the adjacent ports, engaged in trawling for turbot, soles, brill, and other flat fish, for the supply of the London market.

They had been out there for nearly three weeks, their wants being supplied, and the fish they had caught being taken away from them by several large cutters, which came out from Yarmouth laden with ice, in which the fish were packed, and thus conveyed to the Thames, or to the nearest railway terminus—thence to be transported to London, and dispersed by similar means all over the country. It was Sunday: some of the vessels had their sails set and their trawls down, their crews in their dirty week-day dresses standing ready to haul them on board. Other vessels, which had drawn close together, had their sails furled, their anchors down, and their trawl-nets hung up in the rigging to dry. A flag was flying at the mainmast-head on board two of them. The device was a figure with wings, and an open book with golden leaves in its hand, on a blue ground, and underneath, the words "Missions to Seamen." These two vessels were somewhat apart, and boats from the others were pulling towards them. On board one of the other vessels—the *Seagull*—the crew were collected on deck, in their clean clothing, maybe not so neat and new as they might have worn on shore, however. The boat was alongside; the captain came on deck.

"Well, lads, who'll go with me to worship God with our fellow-Christians?" he asked.

"What's come over the old man, of late?" growled out one of the roughest-looking of the crew. "We used to do very well without all this praying and preaching; and I don't see what good it'll do us."

One or two laughed: but no one answered.

"You'll go, father," said a young lad, Robby Starling, addressing another of the men. "You can't tell what beautiful things are said; and then there's praying and singing; it does one's heart good to hear them sing. Come, father; come."

"It's time to shove off, lads," said the old captain, looking round to see who would go.

W. H. G. Kingston

Robby again pleaded with his father, who at length stepped into the boat with two other men, his son, another lad, and the captain.

The weather was calm and fine, so that it allowed of an awning to be stretched over the deck, under which seats were arranged for the accommodation of thirty or forty persons. The sailor missionary, who acted as mate of the missionary fishing-vessel, after appropriate prayers had been offered up and psalms sung, urged his hearers, in a loving manner, to accept the gracious offer of salvation while there was yet time.

All were impressed with this address; no one more so than Rob Starling's father and the other men from the *Sea-gull*. Before leaving the vessel the elder Starling went to the missionary, begged him for his prayers, told him how heartily sorry he was for all his sins, and yet that he was sure his loving Saviour would wash them all away.

Notwithstanding the calmness of the morning, there had been indications all day of a change of weather; and just as the sun went down, the admiral (for so the most experienced captain of the fleet elected to that post is called) hoisted the signal for the vessels to return to port. As the fleet had a week or more to remain out, he had been unwilling to make the signal, though it might have been better had he done so earlier; but even the most experienced are at times mistaken as to the weather at sea.

Those who had been trawling all day hauled their trawls on board; and those which had been brought up, lifted their anchors, and all made sail together.

Before midnight a fierce gale was blowing from the westward, shifting now from the south-west, now from the north-west, and creating a heavy cross-sea. The fishing-vessels took different directions. Some stood to the north, some towards the south, endeavouring, as best they could, to beat up against the gale; but they were quickly dispersed here and there, so that the seamen on board the *Sea-gull*, with which we have to do, when they looked out into the gloom around, could not discover a single sail near them. Dark seas, with white, foaming crests, rose up on every side, threatening to fall over on the deck of the little vessel, and send her to the bottom. Now she rose to the summit of one of them now she sunk down into the deep trough between them; tumbling and pitching as if the sport of their fury. The lightning flashed vividly; the wind howled in the rigging; the waves roared, and ever and anon struck the vessel as if about to batter in her sides, sending the spray flying over her deck, wetting the crew (who stood holding on to the bulwarks or rigging) through and through.

There was a loud crash, followed by a groan: the mizen yard had parted, and, falling, had struck the old master, Captain Snow, to the deck. His men raised him up; he could not speak. He was carried below, where his injuries could be looked to.

"Robby, my son, do you and Bill Cuffe go below, and look after the old man; this is not a night for boys like you to be on deck," said the elder Starling, who now took the command.

The boys gladly obeyed. Bill Cuffe proposed turning into their berths to go to sleep; but Robby said, "No! we were told to look after the captain."

The men, by a sickly light of a lantern, examined the captain's hurts, as he lay in his berth, but though they could not discover that any limb was broken, they soon saw that he

W. H. G. Kingston

was beyond their skill. They had, too, to hurry on deck to help repair the damage to the rigging. Soon after, Robby and Bill Cuffe heard the men on deck battening down the hatches; it was a sign that things were becoming even more serious than at first. The bulkheads below creaked; the seas thumped and thumped against the sides, and the *Sea-gull* tumbled and pitched about in every conceivable manner.

"What's going to happen? ain't we all going to the bottom?" asked Bill. "What shall we do, Robby?"

"Do our duty, Bill, whatever happens, as the missionary told us this morning; and pray to God to take care of us all aboard here," answered Robby. "We've now to try to help the captain; I think I hear him speaking."

The boys went to the captain's side. He had returned to consciousness. "What's happened, boy?" he asked: "I can't move hand or foot." Robby told him. "God's will be done," he murmured. "Your father'll do his best—he's a good seaman. He went to service with us this morning. I wish all had gone."

While he was speaking, the vessel received a more furious blow; then there was a rushing noise of water overhead, followed by loud crashes and a few faint shrieks, and then the vessel seemed to bound upwards, and no other sound was heard but that of the seas which washed against the sides. The boys clung to each other in terror; something dreadful had happened, they had been long enough at sea to know that. They dreaded to ask each other; yet what could those shrieks mean? There were no sound of footsteps on deck; the movement of the vessel was different; she no longer went ahead, but lay tossed about by the sea.

"Boys, are you prepared to meet your God?" asked the

captain, in a deep tone, making an effort to speak. "Pray with me." The boys went to him and knelt by his side. He tried in vain to lift up his hands. They repeated the solemn words he uttered. His speech grew fainter and fainter, then ceased altogether. A few faint groans followed, then there was an ominous silence. Robby held the lantern to the old man's face. The eyes were open, but all expression had gone.

"Speak, Captain Snow; speak, Mr Snow—oh! do—do!" cried the boy. "He's gone—the captain's dead, Bill," he said, sadly, after waiting for some time and getting no answer. "How sorry father and the rest will be!"

The boys had not even then realised what had happened on deck. Again the lugger was wildly tossed about. Another heavy blow was followed by a rush of water below. It seemed to come in forward. They could stand the suspense no longer, but rushing up the companion-ladder, with their united strength they forced back the hatch, and looked out. Better had it been for them, poor boys, had they remained in ignorance till daylight of what had happened.

The masts were gone; the boat was gone; the bulwarks were gone; and not a human being remained on deck. The sea had swept it clear, with the exception of the companion-hatch, which was low and unusually strong. To this they owed their preservation. Had it been carried away, the vessel must soon have filled; as it was, the fore-hatch had lifted, and allowed the water to pour down. Should it be carried away, the vessel would very probably go down. Mechanically drawing over the hatch again, they returned into the cabin, and sat down, sobbing and wringing their hands.

"Perhaps they're gone away in the boat," suggested Bill Cuffe.

W. H. G. Kingston

Hobby for an instant checked his tears, but immediately saw the improbability of this. "Oh, no, no! They're all gone! they're all gone!" he repeated again and again. "No one but us two and the dead captain aboard the craft."

"What shall we do, then?" asked Bill, after a long silence.

Hobby looked at his companion earnestly before speaking. "Trust in God, and do our duty," he said, at length.

"Yes, but what is our duty, Robby?"

"I don't see that we can do much, as yet," answered Robby, "but trust in God, and pray to Him. Yes, I've heard say that when people die, their friends go and shut their eyes: the captain's are open; let's go and do that for him."

Together they went back to the body, and while Bill held the lantern, Robby reverently closed the eyes of the dead man.

The *Sea-gull* continued tumbling about as before, now tossed to the top of one curling wave, now to that of another; while every now and then a fresh rush of water down the fore-hatch made the two boys dread more than ever that she would ere long go to the bottom. They dared not go on deck to see how matters stood, because they knew that if they did they most probably would be swept off it; so they sat down on the floor of the little cabin, and held on by the leg of the table, wishing that daylight would come and the storm cease.

The night seemed a very long one; so, indeed, it was. Wearied out, they at length both slept. How long, they could not tell, but a sudden lurch threw them against the side of the vessel, and they awoke, but with their senses confused, and neither of them able to recollect clearly what had occurred.

The light in their lantern had burnt out, and they were in total darkness.

Suddenly Bill exclaimed, "Oh, Robby, where's the captain?"

"Dead," said Robby: "you haven't forgotten that, surely."

"Dead!" exclaimed Bill. "Oh, so he is, and we two here with him alone in the cabin away out in the open sea. I can't stand it, I tell you. Where shall we go? what shall we do?"

Terror caused by thinking of the supernatural is especially infectious. Robby was but a boy. In spite of his better judgment, he allowed his feelings to get the better of it, and he began to tremble like his companion. This was but natural. Brought up as are boys of his class, who could blame him? There were the two lads, with their dead captain, rolling about in a leaky craft during that fierce gale out in the North Sea. They dared not go on deck; they feared to remain in the cabin: they crept over as far as they could from the side where the dead body lay. Not till Robby again thought of praying did he regain his composure. With the hatches battened down and the skylight covered over, daylight could not penetrate in the little cabin. The boys forgot this, and sat on, Robby at length again falling asleep, but Bill's fears kept him awake. After a time it seemed to him that the vessel did not tumble about so much; he was very hungry also, and he thought that it must be day, and as he was afraid of moving by himself, he awoke Robby, and together they groped their way to the companion-hatch, and, unfastening it, the bright sunlight streamed full on their dazzled eyes. The sea had gone down somewhat, but still it washed over the deck, which was wet and slippery, and so they were afraid to venture on it lest they should be washed off. Hobby looked around, in the faint hope that some one might be yet clinging to the vessel, but not one of the seven men they had left there

W. H. G. Kingston

when they went below remained. Then he scanned the horizon on every side. Foam-crested, dancing waves alone were to be seen. Not a sail appeared. Bill now cried out for food. They could venture to leave the companion-hatch off, and by the light which streamed down it they were able to hunt about for some. They soon found some cold meat and biscuit, and fortunately also a jar of water, and, with these things, quickly appeased their hunger. They had no fear, indeed, of starving, for there were plenty of fish on board, and an ample supply of provisions of all sorts, but the cooking-place was forward, and they could not venture along the deck to get to it. After their meal their spirits improved. Hobby remarked with confidence that, as the vessel had floated so long through the worst part of the gale, she might still weather it out altogether. They could hear, however, by the rushing sound inside as she rolled, that there was a great deal of water in her. "We must try and pump it out," said Robby. To do that they must wait till they could get forward, where the brake of the pump was kept.

All this time the wind was falling and the sea was going down, and at last Robby thought that by working their way along the masts they might reach the forehatch. He led, Bill followed. The hatch was found partially off. Fortunately, it had not been altogether washed away, for, as it was, large quantities of water had got down and damaged everything in the forecastle. Bill, again frightened by the damage the vessel had sustained, thought that pumping would be of no use.

"It's our duty to pump this vessel—and do so I will, if I can," said Robby, firmly.

The pump, not without difficulty, was rigged, and they set to work manfully. It was very hard work too, but it was satisfactory to see the clear water rushing out through the scuppers, and to believe that none was coming in. They pumped and pumped away till they were weary, and then went back into the cabin to lie down awhile.

They had now got more accustomed to the sight of their dead captain, so that even Bill did not object to passing the night in the cabin. The next day they again pumped away, and had entirely freed the vessel by noon. Having nothing more to do, their thoughts turned towards the possibility of reaching England. They anxiously scanned the horizon in the hopes of seeing some vessel approaching them. A sail was seen at length—they thought that she was coming towards them, but she stood away; then another and another came in sight; but their vessel was not perceived. Another night came on. As the sun went down, the sky again became very threatening. Before midnight the gale had returned. There was no compass below, so the boys did not know from what quarter it blew. Poor Bill began really to despair, and wanted to get into a berth and go to sleep till he was drowned.

"No, don't do that," said Robby. "While there's life there's hope; and, depend on't, God knows what's best for us."

The storm raged furiously, but the little vessel, freed from water, and light as a cask, floated like a cork driven before it. At length the gale ceased, and the sea went down, and the two boys went on deck. The coast was in sight—they knew it well—they were off Lowestoft. Boats came off—the *Seagull* was towed into the Yar. It became known how Robby and Bill had kept the vessel afloat by pumping her out before the second gale came on. A subscription was raised for Robby and his mother; and, though he is very young, he commands a vessel of his own, still firm in the belief which he endeavours to impress on others, that "God knows what is best for us."

W. H. G. Kingston

ABOUT THE AUTHOR

William Henry Giles Kingston (1814 - 1880), writer of tales for boys, born in London, but spent much of his youth in Oporto, where his father was a merchant.

His first book, The Circassian Chief, appeared in 1844. His first book for boys, Peter the Whaler, was published in 1851, and had such success that he retired from business and devoted himself entirely to the production of this kind of literature, in which his popularity was deservedly great; and during 30 years he wrote upwards of 130 tales, including The Three Midshipmen (1862), The Three Lieutenants (1874), The Three Commanders (1875), The Three Admirals (1877), Digby Heathcote, etc.

He also conducted various papers, including The Colonist, and Colonial Magazine and East India Review. He was also interested in emigration, volunteering, and various philanthropic schemes. For services in negotiating a commercial treaty with Portugal he received a Portuguese knighthood, and for his literary labours a Government pension.

Choose from Thousands of 1stWorldLibrary Classics By

A. M. Barnard	Booth Tarkington	Edward Everett Hale
Ada Leverson	Boyd Cable	Edward J. O'Biren
Adolphus William Ward	Bram Stoker	Edward S. Ellis
Aesop	C. Collodi	Edwin L. Arnold
Agatha Christie	C. E. Orr	Eleanor Atkins
Alexander Aaronsohn	C. M. Ingleby	Eleanor Hallowell Abbott
Alexander Kielland	Carolyn Wells	Eliot Gregory
Alexandre Dumas	Catherine Parr Traill	Elizabeth Gaskell
Alfred Gatty	Charles A. Eastman	Elizabeth McCracken
Alfred Ollivant	Charles Amory Beach	Elizabeth Von Arnim
Alice Duer Miller	Charles Dickens	Ellem Key
Alice Turner Curtis	Charles Dudley Warner	Emerson Hough
Alice Dunbar	Charles Farrar Browne	Emilie F. Carlen
Allen Chapman	Charles Ives	Emily Bronte
Alleyne Ireland	Charles Kingsley	Emily Dickinson
Ambrose Bierce	Charles Klein	Enid Bagnold
Amelia E. Barr	Charles Hanson Towne	Enilor Macartney Lane
Amory H. Bradford	Charles Lathrop Pack	Erasmus W. Jones
Andrew Lang	Charles Romyn Dake	Ernie Howard Pie
Andrew McFarland Davis	Charles Whibley	Ethel May Dell
Andy Adams	Charles Willing Beale	Ethel Turner
Angela Brazil	Charlotte M. Braeme	Ethel Watts Mumford
Anna Alice Chapin	Charlotte M. Yonge	Eugene Sue
Anna Sewell	Charlotte Perkins Stetson	Eugenie Foa
Annie Besant	Clair W. Hayes	Eugene Wood
Annie Hamilton Donnell	Clarence Day Jr.	Eustace Hale Ball
Annie Payson Call	Clarence E. Mulford	Evelyn Everett-green
Annie Roe Carr	Clemence Housman	Everard Cotes
Annonaymous	Confucius	F. H. Cheley
Anton Chekhov	Coningsby Dawson	F. J. Cross
Archibald Lee Fletcher	Cornelis DeWitt Wilcox	F. Marion Crawford
Arnold Bennett	Cyril Burleigh	Fannie E. Newberry
Arthur C. Benson	D. H. Lawrence	Federick Austin Ogg
Arthur Conan Doyle	Daniel Defoe	Ferdinand Ossendowski
Arthur M. Winfield	David Garnett	Fergus Hume
Arthur Ransome	Dinah Craik	Florence A. Kilpatrick
Arthur Schnitzler	Don Carlos Janes	Fremont B. Deering
Arthur Train	Donald Keyhoe	Francis Bacon
Atticus	Dorothy Kilner	Francis Darwin
B.H. Baden-Powell	Dougan Clark	Frances Hodgson Burnett
B. M. Bower	Douglas Fairbanks	Frances Parkinson Keyes
B. C. Chatterjee	E. Nesbit	Frank Gee Patchin
Baroness Emmuska Orczy	E. P. Roe	Frank Harris
Baroness Orczy	E. Phillips Oppenheim	Frank Jewett Mather
Basil King	E. S. Brooks	Frank L. Packard
Bayard Taylor	Earl Barnes	Frank V. Webster
Ben Macomber	Edgar Rice Burroughs	Frederic Stewart Isham
Bertha Muzzy Bower	Edith Van Dyne	Frederick Trevor Hill
Bjornstjerne Bjornson	Edith Wharton	Frederick Winslow Taylor

Friedrich Kerst
Friedrich Nietzsche
Fyodor Dostoyevsky
G.A. Henty
G.K. Chesterton
Gabrielle E. Jackson
Garrett P. Serviss
Gaston Leroux
George A. Warren
George Ade
Geroge Bernard Shaw
George Cary Eggleston
George Durston
George Ebers
George Eliot
George Gissing
George MacDonald
George Meredith
George Orwell
George Sylvester Viereck
George Tucker
George W. Cable
George Wharton James
Gertrude Atherton
Gordon Casserly
Grace E. King
Grace Gallatin
Grace Greenwood
Grant Allen
Guillermo A. Sherwell
Gulielma Zollinger
Gustav Flaubert
H. A. Cody
H. B. Irving
H.C. Bailey
H. G. Wells
H. H. Munro
H. Irving Hancock
H. R. Naylor
H. Rider Haggard
H. W. C. Davis
Haldeman Julius
Hall Caine
Hamilton Wright Mabie
Hans Christian Andersen
Harold Avery
Harold McGrath
Harriet Beecher Stowe
Harry Castlemon
Harry Coghill
Harry Houidini

Hayden Carruth
Helent Hunt Jackson
Helen Nicolay
Hendrik Conscience
Hendy David Thoreau
Henri Barbusse
Henrik Ibsen
Henry Adams
Henry Ford
Henry Frost
Henry James
Henry Jones Ford
Henry Seton Merriman
Henry W Longfellow
Herbert A. Giles
Herbert Carter
Herbert N. Casson
Herman Hesse
Hildegard G. Frey
Homer
Honore De Balzac
Horace B. Day
Horace Walpole
Horatio Alger Jr.
Howard Pyle
Howard R. Garis
Hugh Lofting
Hugh Walpole
Humphry Ward
Ian Maclaren
Inez Haynes Gillmore
Irving Bacheller
Isabel Cecilia Williams
Isabel Hornibrook
Israel Abrahams
Ivan Turgenev
J.G.Austin
J. Henri Fabre
J. M. Barrie
J. M. Walsh
J. Macdonald Oxley
J. R. Miller
J. S. Fletcher
J. S. Knowles
J. Storer Clouston
J. W. Duffield
Jack London
Jacob Abbott
James Allen
James Andrews
James Baldwin

James Branch Cabell
James DeMille
James Joyce
James Lane Allen
James Lane Allen
James Oliver Curwood
James Oppenheim
James Otis
James R. Driscoll
Jane Abbott
Jane Austen
Jane L. Stewart
Janet Aldridge
Jens Peter Jacobsen
Jerome K. Jerome
Jessie Graham Flower
John Buchan
John Burroughs
John Cournos
John F. Kennedy
John Gay
John Glasworthy
John Habberton
John Joy Bell
John Kendrick Bangs
John Milton
John Philip Sousa
John Taintor Foote
Jonas Lauritz Idemil Lie
Jonathan Swift
Joseph A. Altsheler
Joseph Carey
Joseph Conrad
Joseph E. Badger Jr
Joseph Hergesheimer
Joseph Jacobs
Jules Vernes
Julian Hawthrone
Julie A Lippmann
Justin Huntly McCarthy
Kakuzo Okakura
Karle Wilson Baker
Kate Chopin
Kenneth Grahame
Kenneth McGaffey
Kate Langley Bosher
Kate Langley Bosher
Katherine Cecil Thurston
Katherine Stokes
L. A. Abbot
L. T. Meade

L. Frank Baum
Latta Griswold
Laura Dent Crane
Laura Lee Hope
Laurence Housman
Lawrence Beasley
Leo Tolstoy
Leonid Andreyev
Lewis Carroll
Lewis Sperry Chafer
Lilian Bell
Lloyd Osbourne
Louis Hughes
Louis Joseph Vance
Louis Tracy
Louisa May Alcott
Lucy Fitch Perkins
Lucy Maud Montgomery
Luther Benson
Lydia Miller Middleton
Lyndon Orr
M. Corvus
M. H. Adams
Margaret E. Sangster
Margret Howth
Margaret Vandercook
Margaret W. Hungerford
Margret Penrose
Maria Edgeworth
Maria Thompson Daviess
Mariano Azuela
Marion Polk Angellotti
Mark Overton
Mark Twain
Mary Austin
Mary Catherine Crowley
Mary Cole
Mary Hastings Bradley
Mary Roberts Rinehart
Mary Rowlandson
M. Wollstonecraft Shelley
Maud Lindsay
Max Beerbohm
Myra Kelly
Nathaniel Hawthrone
Nicolo Machiavelli
O. F. Walton
Oscar Wilde

Owen Johnson
P.G. Wodehouse
Paul and Mabel Thorne
Paul G. Tomlinson
Paul Severing
Percy Brebner
Percy Keese Fitzhugh
Peter B. Kyne
Plato
Quincy Allen
R. Derby Holmes
R. L. Stevenson
R. S. Ball
Rabindranath Tagore
Rahul Alvares
Ralph Bonehill
Ralph Henry Barbour
Ralph Victor
Ralph Waldo Emmerson
Rene Descartes
Ray Cummings
Rex Beach
Rex E. Beach
Richard Harding Davis
Richard Jefferies
Richard Le Gallienne
Robert Barr
Robert Frost
Robert Gordon Anderson
Robert L. Drake
Robert Lansing
Robert Lynd
Robert Michael Ballantyne
Robert W. Chambers
Rosa Nouchette Carey
Rudyard Kipling
Saint Augustine
Samuel B. Allison
Samuel Hopkins Adams
Sarah Bernhardt
Sarah C. Hallowell
Selma Lagerlof
Sherwood Anderson
Sigmund Freud
Standish O'Grady
Stanley Weyman
Stella Benson
Stella M. Francis

Stephen Crane
Stewart Edward White
Stijn Streuvels
Swami Abhedananda
Swami Parmananda
T. S. Ackland
T. S. Arthur
The Princess Der Ling
Thomas A. Janvier
Thomas A Kempis
Thomas Anderton
Thomas Bailey Aldrich
Thomas Bulfinch
Thomas De Quincey
Thomas Dixon
Thomas H. Huxley
Thomas Hardy
Thomas More
Thornton W. Burgess
U. S. Grant
Upton Sinclair
Valentine Williams
Various Authors
Vaughan Kester
Victor Appleton
Victor G. Durham
Victoria Cross
Virginia Woolf
Wadsworth Camp
Walter Camp
Walter Scott
Washington Irving
Wilbur Lawton
Wilkie Collins
Willa Cather
Willard F. Baker
William Dean Howells
William le Queux
W. Makepeace Thackeray
William W. Walter
William Shakespeare
Winston Churchill
Yei Theodora Ozaki
Yogi Ramacharaka
Young E. Allison
Zane Grey

www.ingramcontent.com/pod-product-compliance
Lightning Source LLC
Chambersburg PA
CBHW031846170626
46807CB00004B/1640